The Speech Sounds of English: Phonetics, Phonology, and Phoneme Awareness

LETRS

Language Essentials for Teachers of Reading and Spelling

Louisa C. Moats, Ed.D.

SOPRIS WEST EDUCATIONAL SERVICES
A CAMBIUM LEARNING COMPANY

BOSTON, MA • NEW YORK, NY • LONGMONT, CO

09 08 07 06 05 04   6 5 4 3 2

Edited by Sandra L. Knauke
Cover design and text layout by Sue Campbell
Slide design by Christine Kosmicki
Production assistance by Sherri Rowe and Kim Harris

ISBN 1-59318-190-6

Printed in the United States of America

Published and Distributed by

SOPRIS
WEST
EDUCATIONAL SERVICES

4093 Specialty Place • Longmont, CO 80504 • (303) 651-2829
www.sopriswest.com

191MOD2/7-04/BAN

Dedication

To my husband, Steve Mitchell, whose support is constant and invaluable.

Acknowledgments

The LETRS modules have been developed with the help of many people. Our active national trainers, including Carol Tolman, Susan Hall, Marcia Davidson, Anne Cunningham, Marcia Berger, Deb Glaser, Linda Farrell, Judi Dodson, and Anne Whitney have all offered valuable suggestions for improving the module content and structure. Their devotion to delivering LETRS across the country is appreciated beyond measure. Bruce Rosow, Kevin Feldman, Susan Lowell, Patricia Mathes, Marianne Steverson, Lynn Kuhn, Jan Hasbrouck, and Nancy Eberhardt contributed their expertise to the first edition and continue to provide essential input and feedback. Many other professionals from all over the country who have attended institutes and offered constructive criticism have enabled our response to educators. I hope you see your ideas reflected in the revised editions of this continually evolving material.

I am grateful for the daily support and energy of the Sopris West office staff, editors, and designers including Lynne Stair, Sue Campbell, Sandra Knauke, Christine Kosmicki, and Kim Harris. Special thanks are due to Toni Backstrom, who manages the LETRS program with enthusiasm, competence, and commitment.

Stu Horsfall, Ray Beck, Steve Mitchell, Chet Foraker, and Steve Kukic are the vision and energy behind the publication of evidence-based programs in education that will help all children learn. I am so fortunate to be working with all of you.

—LCM

Contents for Module 2

Overview of LETRS: Language Essentials for Teachers of Reading and Spelling

LETRS is designed to enrich and extend, but not to replace, program-specific professional development for teachers of reading and language arts. Teachers who implement a core, comprehensive reading program must know the format and instructional routines necessary to implement daily lessons. Teaching reading is complex and demanding, and new teachers will need both modeling and classroom coaching to implement the program well. Program-specific training, however, is not enough to enable teachers to tailor instruction to the diverse needs in their classrooms. Even teachers who are getting good results will need to understand the research-based principles of reading development, reading differences, and reading instruction. Reaching *all* learners through assessment and intervention is only possible when the teacher understands who is having difficulty, why they might be struggling, and what approaches to intervention are grounded in evidence. An empowered teacher is one who knows and can implement the best practices of the field, as established by a scientific research consensus.

The American Federation of Teachers' *Teaching Reading Is Rocket Science* and the Learning First Alliance's *Every Child Reading: A Professional Development Guide* provided the blueprint for these modules. LETRS modules teach concepts about language structure, reading development, reading difficulty, and assessment practices that guide research-based instruction. The format of instruction in LETRS allows for deep learning and reflection beyond the brief "once over" treatment the topics are typically given. Our professional development approach has been successful with diverse groups of teachers: regular classroom and special education, novice and expert, rural and urban.

The modules address each component of reading instruction in depth—phonological and phonemic awareness; phonics, decoding, spelling, and word study; oral language development; vocabulary; reading fluency; comprehension; and writing—as well as the links among these components. The characteristics and the needs of second language learners (ELL), dialect speakers, and students with other learning differences are woven into the modules. Assessment modules teach a problem-solving strategy for grouping children and designing instruction.

Teachers usually need extended time to learn and apply the knowledge and skills included in LETRS, depending on their background and experience. The content is dense by design. Each module is written so that teacher participants will engage in questions, problems, and tasks that lead to understanding, but understanding may occur in small steps, gradually, over several years. Some of the modules also are accompanied by the LETRS Interactive CD-ROMS, self-instructional supplements for independent study and practice, developed with the help of a grant from

the SBIR program of the National Institute for Child Health and Human Development.

More information about LETRS material, programs, and institutes is available at www.letrs.com.

Content of LETRS Modules Within the Language-Literacy Connection

Components of Comprehensive Reading Instruction	Organization of Language						
	Phonology	Morphology	Orthography	Semantics	Syntax	Discourse and Pragmatics	Etymology
Phonological Awareness	2	2					
Phonics, Spelling, and Word Study	3, 7	3, 7, 10	3, 7, 10				3, 10
Fluency	5		5	5	5		
Vocabulary	4	4	4	4	4		4
Text Comprehension		6		6	6	6, 11	
Written Expression			9, 11	9, 11	9, 11	9, 11	
Assessment	8, 12	8, 12	8, 12	8, 12	8, 12	8, 12	

Note: Each module is identified by number; there are 12 modules in development.

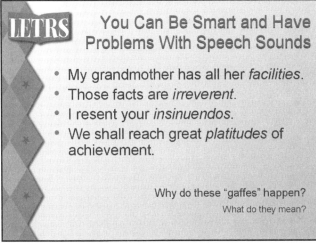

You Can Be Smart and Have Problems With Speech Sounds

- My grandmother has all her *facilities*.
- Those facts are *irreverent*.
- I resent your *insinuendos*.
- We shall reach great *platitudes* of achievement.

Why do these "gaffes" happen?
What do they mean?

Slide 2

Language Systems Are Distinct

- Phonetics: the inventory of speech sounds
- Phonology: the use of phonemes in words
- Phonics: sound-symbol associations
- Orthography: the spelling system
- Morphology: the meaningful parts of words
- Semantics: word or phrase meanings
- Syntax: the rules of sentence structure

Slide 3

Objectives

♦ Respond to a range of phonological tasks.

♦ Explain the relationship between phoneme awareness, phonological processing, and phonics.

♦ Define, identify, and segment important linguistic units including vowels, consonants, syllables, and onset-rime.

♦ After practice with a model, pronounce the vowel and consonant phonemes.

♦ Achieve 90% accuracy with matching, producing, counting, blending, segmenting, and manipulating phonemes in one-syllable words.

♦ Recognize phonological influences on children's inventive spelling.

♦ Review the phonemes of Spanish and the way they differ from English, and recognize that most dialect differences are rule-based.

The "Ph" Words

What is the difference between the terms *phonological processing, phonetics, phoneme awareness*, and *phonics*? Only those who have some formal training in linguistics—such as speech/language therapists, voice and diction teachers, or students of the world's languages—are likely to know! The terms refer to different concepts and are not interchangeable. They all pertain to unique aspects of language processing that play a central role in learning to read, spell, and write.

The term *auditory* is too vague and general to help us differentiate these terms. Each "ph" word, however, does describe an auditory function. The root *phon* in the words *phonological, phonetic, phonemic*, and *phonic* is derived from the Latin root for "sound." Phonological, phonetic, phonemic, and phonic information, however, is first and foremost *linguistic*. The notes of a symphony, the clang of a garbage can lid, and the roar of a sea lion are auditory but not linguistic. Networks in the brain that process environmental sounds are distinct from those networks responsible for language comprehension and production. Moreover, language itself has special properties, including several rule systems and underlying structures, that each requires its own specialized neural networks. Each language system is modular, and each language system is vulnerable to developmental problems.

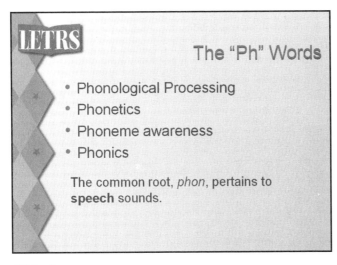

The "Ph" Words

- Phonological Processing
- Phonetics
- Phoneme awareness
- Phonics

The common root, *phon*, pertains to **speech** sounds.

Slide 4

Phonological Processing

Phonological processing is a huge topic! Phonological processing refers to many aspects of speech and language perception and production. Phonological processing entails multiple functions, such as perceiving, interpreting, storing (remembering), recalling or retrieving, and generating the speech sound system of a language. It is a processing system used for such seemingly diverse tasks as

© The New Yorker Collection 2001 William Haefeli. Reprinted with permission.

"You have the wrong number. No one whose name is pronounced that way lives here."

repeating a series of random numbers, imitating the pronunciation of a word we have never heard before, producing new sounds in an unfamiliar language, or searching our memory for a word to use in a sentence.

Researchers have often observed that people tend to perform similarly on tests that measure diverse aspects of phonological processing, and thus have proposed that phonological skill is a language capability that can be demonstrated in a number of ways. For example, an individual may be good or poor at all of these tasks: repeating nonsense words, taking words apart into their individual speech sounds (phoneme segmentation), and speaking Pig Latin. Reading scientists have discovered that people with reading and spelling problems tend to have trouble with a variety of phonological tasks, including the association of speech sounds with symbols. Likewise, it is true that individuals who have trouble with phonological tasks are likely to be poor readers and spellers.

This fact is well proven: Phonological skill is critical for learning to read any alphabetic writing system. Phonological skill is even important for reading other kinds of writing systems, such as Chinese and Japanese. Dozens of studies indicate that performance on phonological tests in kindergarten and beginning first grade, in combination with letter naming, predict to a great extent who will learn to read well, who is likely to read poorly, and who is going to be a good or poor speller.

On the other hand, phonological skill is not strongly related to intelligence. Some very intelligent people (even prominent political leaders!) have trouble with English language structure, especially at the phonological level. Take heart: If you find any of the following tasks challenging, you may be competent in many other ways!

> J.S. Bach was a virtuoso who played many concerts and had many children.
> In between, he practiced in the attic on a spinster.[1]—*Anguished English*

[1] Adapted from Lederer, 1987.

LETRS Exercise Your Phonological Skill

1. Syllable counting
2. Rhyme recognition
3. Word pronunciation
4. Odd word out
5. Phoneme matching

6. Initial phoneme isolation
7. Phoneme blending
8. Phoneme segmentation
9. Phoneme deletion
10. Phoneme sequence identification

Slide 5

Exercise #1: Various Phonological Tasks

Try these phonological processing tasks.

1. (Syllable Counting) How many syllables in each of the following words?

   cleaned _____   poetic _____   appreciated _____   incredible _____

2. (Rhyme Recognition) Do each of these word pairs rhyme (yes or no)? Speakers may differ in their judgments.

   but, putt _____   been, when _____   loyal, toil _____

   merry, scary _____   on, yawn _____

3. (Word Pronunciation) How do you pronounce each of these words? On which ones might you reveal your regional or ethnic origins?

   tomato ☐   parker ☐   oil ☐   caught ☐   wash ☐   sing ☐

4. (Odd Word Out) Which word does not begin with the same sound as the others?

   theory ☐   therefore ☐   thistle ☐   thinker ☐

Module 2

The Speech Sounds of English: Phonetics, Phonology, and Phoneme Awareness

(continued) **Exercise #1:** Various Phonological Tasks

5. (Phoneme Matching). Which word has the same last sound as *does*?

    miss ☐   nice ☐   prize ☐   purchase ☐

6. (Initial Phoneme Isolation) Say the first speech sound in each of these words:

    europe _____   chagrin _____   psychic _____   question _____

7. (Phoneme Blending) Blend these sounds together to make a whole, real word:

    /th/ /ŭ/ /m/ _____   /s/ /t/ /ǎ/ /k/ /s/ _____

    /m/ /or/ /f/ /ē/ /m/ _____   /y/ /ū/ /n/ [ə] /v/ /er/ /s/ _____

8. (Phoneme Segmentation) Raise a finger for each sound as you break each word into its individual speech sounds (phonemes).

    shear   chains   quite   fleshy

9. (Phoneme Deletion)

    Say *driver*. Say it again without the /v/.   _____

    Say *smoke*. Say it again without the /m/.   _____

    Say *sink*. Say it again without the /ŋ/.   _____

    Say *six*. Say it again without the /k/.   _____

10. (Phoneme Sequence Identification) What is the third speech sound in each of these words?

    chunk _____   writhe _____   vision _____   exit _____

8

Repetition of long or unfamiliar words, judgment of rhyme, counting of syllables and speech sounds, blending of speech sounds, repetition of sentences or numbers, and matching speech sounds can all be accomplished without knowing the meaning of a word or how to spell it. Thus, these tasks all place direct demands on the phonological processor. To remember a sentence and repeat it, our understanding of the meaning and sentence pattern may help us recall the words, but the act of repeating a sentence verbatim demands phonological memory.

The exercises just practiced are not easy for many people. Our minds are not used to focusing specifically on speech sounds in words. The phonological processor likes to do its job without calling attention to itself. It is designed to extract the meaning of what is said, not to focus consciously on the speech sounds in the words. It is supposed to do its job *automatically*, without getting in the way of efficient communication. That's why we *use* speech sounds without necessarily knowing what they are, and why teachers have to study the sounds to be consciously aware of them.

Phonology and Memory for Speech

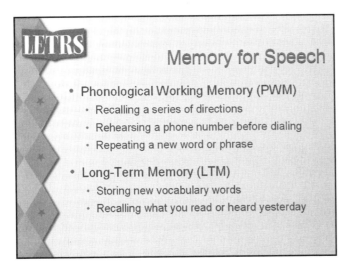

Slide 6

When we listen to language and extract meaning, we store the incoming language in temporary or **phonological working memory (PWM)**. Phonological working memory is like the looping tape that was used for telephone answering machines: it has a limited amount of storage space and it gets "taped over" constantly as we comprehend speech. We give it a workout when we try to remember a telephone number long enough to write it down; remember the directions we just got to a destination; or hold what we just read in mind while we read the next section of a book. Children who seem "spacey" or "forgetful" in these ways often have problems with phonological working memory.

We place demands on PWM when we ask students to retell what they have heard, to follow a series of directions, or to repeat sentences before writing them down. Only some of what we hear or read is extracted from PWM and sent to storage in **long-term memory** (LTM).

When we speak, we draw words from our **lexicons** or mental dictionaries, pop them into the sentence structures that will convey our intended meaning, and articulate the sounds so that a listener who speaks the same language can understand. The lexicon is the stored word bank in LTM. Words filed in the lexicon are phonological entities as well as units of meaning with assigned grammatical roles. We know the difference between *put* and *putt* because the words have different phonemes. Similarly, we know that *gas*, *glass*, and *grass* are separate words.

Words have to be **retrieved** from long-term memory to be spoken. When we pass a child we know in the hall and can't remember his or her name, a phonological form in long-term memory has temporarily eluded our mental search process. We know it's there, but we can't get it out. Failure to retrieve words may be due to faulty storage of the word image in the first place, or to a faulty search and recall process.

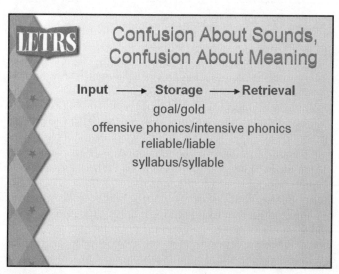

Slide 7

Imagine trying to remember a new word you just heard such as *dysdiodochokinesia*. When the sounds in words are coded for long-term storage, the quality of the memory formed will depend on the attention given to those sounds, the accuracy with which the sounds were perceived, and the strategies employed to find a "filing slot" in memory from which that word or name can be retrieved. People who have trouble remembering words exactly as they first heard them are often affected by a more fundamental inability to form a complete, accurate image of all the sounds in the word.[2] If a person thinks that *goal* is the same as *gold* or that *dyslexia* is *dylelia*, communication may be sabotaged.

---

[2] Fuller explanations of these phenomena by a leading researcher in phonological memory processes can be found in Brady, 1997.

The Speech Sounds of English: Phonetics, Phonology, and Phoneme Awareness

Phonological processing is a part of word learning at several levels:

♦ "Hearing" or being aware of the sounds in words.

♦ Pronouncing words.

♦ Remembering words accurately.

♦ Differentiating words that sound similar.

> " . . . My sisters gawked at the fascinating stranger and hung on his every
> syllabus of English . . . "—*The Poisonwood Bible*, p. 128[3]

Thus, the phonological problems that poor readers often experience may undermine their ability to do a range of language tasks, such as follow lengthy directions; remember lists of things such as states and capitols; learn vocabulary words readily by hearing them in context; remember the names of characters from stories, the labels for body parts, or the names of historical places; and recall the sounds that match up with letters and letter sequences.

Exercise #2: Repeat a Foreign Language

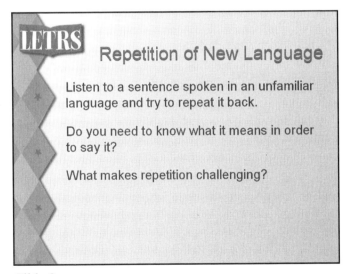

Slide 8

Listen to a phrase or sentence spoken in an unfamiliar language and try to repeat it back. Is this easy or difficult for you? Do you need to know what it means in order to say it? What makes repetition challenging?

---

[3] Kingsolver, Barbara. (1999). *The Poisonwood Bible*. New York: HarperCollins.

Under the Phonological Umbrella

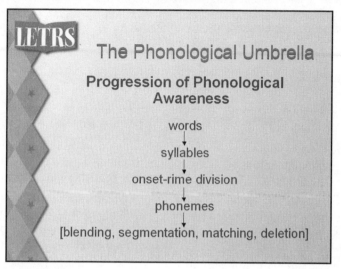

Slide 9

Phonological awareness is an umbrella concept under which the concept of **phonemic awareness** can be found. Phonemic awareness refers to one aspect of phonological skill: awareness of the individual speech sounds (consonants and vowels) in spoken syllables and the ability to manipulate those sounds.

Phonological awareness is a term that includes, in addition to phoneme awareness, the ability to identify, count, and manipulate other linguistic units that are larger than the phoneme. These are:

◆ **Syllables**—units of speech organized around a vowel sound that can include consonants before or after the vowel.

> man – eu – ver
> dis – or – gan – i – za – tion

◆ **Onset-rime units**—units that occur if a syllable is divided into two parts. The consonants before the vowel are the onset, and the vowel plus any additional consonants are the rime.

> f – ish
> fr – esh
> squ – ish
> spl – ash

Note that *rime* is the name for part of a syllable, whereas *rhyme* is the activity of matching words by their rimes.

Exercise #3: Segmenting Words at Several Levels

How are these words divided? By syllable (S), onset-rime (O/R), or phoneme (P)?

h – ou – se	_____	side – walk	_____
f – igh – t	_____	st – age	_____
shr – imp	_____	m – eat	_____
an – i – mal	_____	th – u – mb	_____
po – ta – to	_____	t – r – ee	_____
air – plane	_____	sh – oe	_____

Why Phoneme Awareness Is So Important

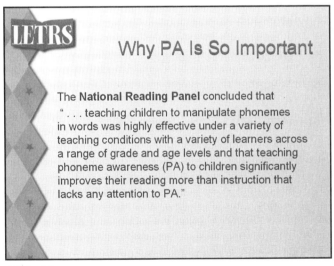

Slide 10

PA Predicts Reading Development

Phoneme awareness has assumed great importance in reading instruction because many research studies have concluded that phoneme awareness is necessary for students to read and write an alphabetic orthography. The National Reading Panel found over 50 scientifically credible studies documenting the importance of phoneme awareness for learning to read and the importance of phoneme awareness instruction for preventing and treating reading difficulties.[4] That is an enormous and irrefutable body of evidence!

---

[4] National Reading Panel, 2000.

© The New Yorker Collection 1993 Mischa Richter. Reprinted with permission.

Several kinds of phonological tasks predict the ability to read, spell, and write, but phoneme awareness is consistently the best predictor. That is, the ability to take a word apart into its component speech sounds and blend those speech sounds together is causally related to success in beginning reading. Further, phonological awareness and the links between sounds and symbols can be directly taught. Finally, when those skills are systematically taught, children have the best chance to "break the code" in early reading, and a better chance to learn how to spell in the early stages. Phoneme awareness is an understanding or insight about words that enables a learner to match graphemes to discrete sounds (phonemes). Some children have much more ability than others to "hear" the internal details of a spoken word, although phoneme awareness depends on much more than hearing. Many children can hear well and can even tell us the names of alphabet letters, but they have little or no idea what those letters represent. Such children, if asked to give the first sound in the word *dog*, are likely to say "woof-woof!" Phoneme awareness underlies the ability to use phonic knowledge to decode unfamiliar words.

Use of Phonics Requires Phoneme Awareness

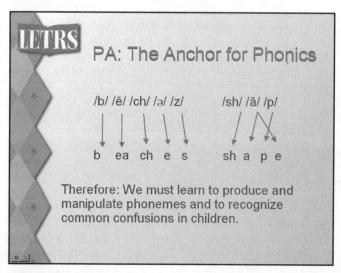

Slide 11

Phoneme awareness provides the foundation on which **phonics** learning is built. Children without phoneme awareness may not understand a teacher's request to say the beginning sound in the words *lit*, *land*, and *lock*. These children may not even know what is meant by the term *sound*. Children must be able to identify /l/ in the words *lit*, *land*, and *lock* and separate the phoneme from others before they will understand what the letter *l* represents in those words. When it is linked

appropriately to sound-symbol association, explicit instruction in sound identification, matching, segmentation, and blending increases the likelihood that children will learn to read and spell.

Thus, teachers must learn enough about speech sounds to pronounce them, link the letters, and recognize students' confusions. Explicit, conscious, and organized knowledge of speech sounds is indispensable for explicit teaching of the alphabetic principle for both reading and spelling.

Exercise #4: Define the PH Words

Explain in your own words the distinctions among phonological processing, phoneme awareness, and phonics.

_____

_____

_____

_____

_____

_____

_____

_____

Key Vocabulary for Module 2
[From the Glossary in the back of the book]

Coarticulation: Speaking phonemes together so that the features of each spreads to neighboring phonemes and all the segments are joined into one linguistic unit (a syllable)

Onset-rime: The natural division of a syllable into two parts, the onset coming before the vowel and the rime including the vowel and what follows it (pl-an, shr-ill)

Phoneme awareness: The conscious awareness that words are made up of segments of our own speech that are represented with letters in an alphabetic orthography

Phonics: The study of the relationships between letters and the sounds they represent; also used as a descriptor for code-based instruction in reading, i.e., "the phonics approach" or "phonic reading"

Phonological processor: A neural network in the frontal and temporal areas of the brain usually the left cerebral hemisphere, that is specialized for speech sound perception, memory, retrieval, and pronunciation

Syllable: The unit of pronunciation that is organized around a vowel; it may or may not have consonants before or after the vowel

The Sequence of English PA Development

LETRS
PA Benchmarks Between Ages 4–9

Typical Age	Skill Domain
4	Rhyme, alliteration.
5	Rhyme, phoneme matching, syllables.
5.5	Onset-rime, initial consonant isolation.
6	Phoneme blending, segmentation (simple).
6.5	Phoneme segmentation, blending, substitution.
7	Initial and final sound deletion.
8	Deletion with blends.
9	Longer and more complex deletion tasks.

Slide 12

Many studies of phonological development point to the following benchmarks for children's progress in this critical skill.[5] Children's performance on phonological tasks can be accelerated through direct teaching and practice. The age at which they consolidate skill will depend, however, on language exposure prior to school, home language context, familiarity with letter-sound correspondence, and overall verbal proficiency.

PA Benchmarks Between Ages 4–9

Typical Age Attained	Skill Domain	Sample Tasks
4	Production and enjoyment of rhyme and alliteration.	Pool, drool, tool . . . Seven silly snakes sang songs seriously.
5	Rhyming, odd word out. Recognition of phonemic changes in words. Clapping, counting syllables.	Which two words rhyme? *stair, steel, chair* "*Hickory Dickory Clock*" isn't right. What should it be? *truck* (1), *airplane* (2), *boat* (1), *automobile* (4)
5.5	Distinguishing and remembering separate phonemes in a series. Blending onset and rime. Segmenting initial sound.	Showing sequences of single phonemes with colored blocks /s/ /s/ /f/; /z/ /sh/ /z/. What word? *th–under*; *qu–een*; *h–appy* Say the first sound in *shoelace*; *sock*; *funnel*.
6	Syllable deletion Compound word deletion. Onset-rime blending; beginning phoneme blending. Phoneme segmentation, simple syllables with 2–3 phonemes [no blends].	Say *parsnip*; say it again but don't say *par*. Say *cowboy*. Say it again but don't say *cow*. /sh/–op (shop) /kw/–ēn (queen) /b/–ā th (bathe) /b/–/ā/–/th/ (bathe) Say the word as you move a chip for each sound: *sh–e*, *m–a–n, l–e–g*

---

[5] Numerous studies suggest a predictable sequence of phonological skill development. Syntheses and overviews of those studies can be found in Rath, 2001, and Goswami, 2000. The sequence is embodied in Adams et al., 1997.

PA Benchmarks Between Ages 4–9 (continued)

Typical Age Attained	Skill Domain	Sample Tasks
6.5	Phoneme segmentation up to 3–4 phonemes, including blends. Phoneme substitution to build new words—simple syllables with no blends.	Say the word slowly while you tap the sounds: b-a-ck, ch-ee-se, c-l-ou-d. Change the /j/ in *cage* to /n/. Change the /ā/ in *cane* to /ō/.
7	Sound deletion, initial and final position.	Say *meat*. Say it again without the /m/. Say *safe*. Say it again without the /f/.
8	Sound deletion, initial position, including blends.	Say *prank*. Now say it again without the /p/.
9	Sound deletion, medial and final blend position.	Say *snail*. Say it again without the /n/. Say *fork*. Say it again without the /k/.

Teaching Phonological Skill: General Principles

General Principles—Teaching PA

- Brief [10–15 minutes], distributed, frequent lessons.
- Two to three activities within a lesson.
- Goal is phoneme segmentation/blending by first grade.
- Gradually move through the developmental progression of task difficulty.
- Oral production of sounds and words is critical.
- Model, lead, observe (I do one, we do one, you do one!).
- Give immediate corrective feedback.
- Touch, move, say—multisensory engagement.
- Transition to letters as appropriate.

Slide 13

Phonological awareness activities should be brief (thirty seconds to three minutes) and playful. They focus on oral language and speech sounds before

those sounds are connected to letters. Children should actively respond with their voices, hands, and bodies; passive listening or silent marking of worksheets does not develop PA. For example, during oral blending of sounds, students can sweep their hand from left to right as they say the blended word. During sound identification activities, children can hold up a card or put their thumbs up.

In kindergarten, phoneme awareness instruction that prepares children for reading takes about 10–15 minutes per day, adding up to a total of twelve to twenty hours of instruction across three to five months. In first grade, phoneme awareness should be taught directly as a warm-up or precursor to direct instruction on sound-symbol correspondences, word identification, and spelling. PA should be revisited at any level when learners are unsure of the sounds in words, especially during spelling lessons.

To summarize these principles:

◆ Teach brief lessons, 10–15 minutes per day.

◆ Two or three focused activities per day are sufficient.

◆ The goal is to build proficiency at segmenting and blending individual phonemes in two- to three-phoneme words.

◆ Gradually move through the developmental progression of task difficulty. The object is to "roam around in phonological space" at the appropriate level of difficulty.

◆ Emphasize oral production of words, syllables, and sounds. After hearing the sounds, children should say them, paying attention to how the sounds feel when they are formed.

◆ Always show children what you want them to do [model]. Do one together, and then let the children do one.

◆ Give immediate corrective feedback. For example, if the child gives a letter name instead of a sound, tell him or her the difference and elicit the correct response.

◆ Think "multisensory": Use concrete objects—such as fingers, chips, blocks, coins, or felts—to represent speech sounds. Inject movement into the activity.

◆ Letters reinforce awareness once children have the idea. PA, reading, and spelling are reciprocal; each benefits the others.

Discover the Speech Sounds of English

LETRS Exercise #5: Counting Phonemes

• Listen to the words as they are spoken.
• Tap out the sounds by touching your thumb to each finger in succession as you say each individual phoneme.
• Then, hold up the number of fingers that corresponds to the number of phonemes in the word.

Slide 14

Exercise #5: Count Phonemes in Words

Try counting the speech sounds in each of these words. Tap out the sounds with your thumb and fingers as you say them separately. We expect you to be unsure of some of the words!

string ____   joyless ____   dodge ____   mixed ____   heard ____

hippo ____   although ____   chew ____   house ____

Counting speech sounds in these words can be challenging. Usually, adults do not agree when they do this exercise, even though these are simple, common words that are likely to be taught in the primary grades. Disagreements may occur because adults tend to pay attention to spelling more than to speech sounds, they have learned contradictory ways of classifying sounds, or they simply have not been taught the inventory of sounds. Consciously knowing the phoneme inventory is unnecessary to speak a language; it is only necessary for teaching a few subjects, including beginning reading and spelling.

Children Confuse Similar Sounds

The reason why the consonants and vowels are presented according to their features of articulation is that children often confuse the speech sounds that share features. That is, they confuse the sounds that sound or feel alike. An expert teacher knows which sounds are similar and confusable, and helps children straighten them out.

Children who benefit most from direct teaching of phoneme awareness have trouble figuring out on their own the identity of individual phonemes, especially

Children Confuse Consonant Sounds That Are Alike

EF̲RY	every	voiceless for voiced fricative
INE̲MS	items	nasal for a stop
GAT̲	grade	omission of /r/ from blend; voiceless for a voiced stop
BAG̲	back	voiced for a voiceless stop
M̲D	bed	nasal for a stop

Slide 15

when they are embedded in whole words. Many children speak and hear whole words without discovering the specific sounds that are in them. Thus, children may not attend closely enough to hear the difference between *close* and *closed*, *shock* and *shark*, or *sis* and *six*. This is why LETRS teaches the entire *system* of phonemes, including their similarities and differences. This knowledge affords valuable insights into why children have trouble distinguishing certain sounds, words, and spellings, and helps the teacher know what examples of sounds and words to choose during instruction. This is also why teachers should be able to say the sounds and model standard production while they are teaching.

What Makes a Consonant?

Consonant Phoneme Chart

Consonant Phonemes by Place and Manner of Articulation

	Lips	Teeth/ Lips	Tongue/ Teeth	Ridge/ Teeth	Roof Mouth	Back of Throat	Glottis
Stops Unvoiced / Voiced	/p/ /b/			/t/ /d/		/k/ /g/	
Nasals	/m/			/n/		/ng/	
Fricatives Unvoiced / Voiced		/f/ /v/	/th/ /th/	/s/ /z/	/sh/ /zh/		
Affricates Unvoiced / Voiced					/ch/ /j/		
Glides Unvoiced / Voiced					/y/	/wh/ /w/	/h/
Liquids				/l/ /r/			

Slide 16

In this module, the word **consonant** is used to refer to a phoneme, not a letter. Consonants are a group of speech sounds that contrast with vowels. They are called the "closed" sounds because they are formed with the vocal airflow partially obstructed. Some consonants, however, have vowel-like qualities and not all consonants are equally accessible in spoken language. For both adults and children, some consonants are harder than others to perceive, pronounce, and unglue from the speech sounds around them.

Look at the "Consonant Phonemes by Place and Manner of Articulation" chart. Any phoneme can be described as a cluster of acoustic features that are produced during articulation. For example, a consonant may be **voiced** (spoken with the vocal cords resonating) or **unvoiced** (spoken with the vocal cords disengaged); **nasal** (spoken with resonance in the nose) or **oral** (with no nasal resonance); a **stop** (with a stop of the airflow) or **continuant** (held as long as the breath lasts). A cluster of such features distinguishes any phoneme in a language.

The 25 consonants on our chart are arranged to show similarities in the way they are articulated. Consonants that are in the same row share features having to do with the manner in which they are pronounced. Consonants that are in the same column share a place of articulation—front, middle, or back of the mouth.

The Consonants, Front to Back

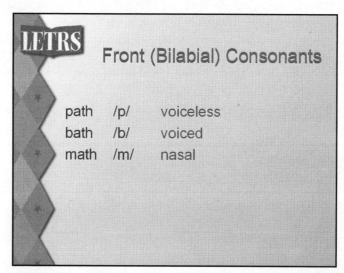

Slide 17

In the front of the mouth, we make three consonants by bringing both lips together. Two of these are stops, /b/ and /p/, and one is a nasal, /m/. Stops are made with one burst of sound. They stand in contrast to continuants, such as the nasal /m/, that can be held until the breath runs out.[6]

---

[6] Many linguistics texts such as Fromkin and Rodman (1998) classify the nasal sounds as stops. For instructional purposes, however, the nasals can be held, stretched out, or exaggerated so that they are easier to blend with other sounds.

Use this blank consonant chart to take notes and construct the consonant inventory with the presenter. See if you can feel your mouth position changing as you say each consonant.

Consonant Phonemes by Place and Manner of Articulation

	Lips	Teeth/ Lips	Tongue/ Teeth	Ridge/ Teeth	Roof of Mouth	Back of Throat	Glottis
Stops Unvoiced / Voiced							
Nasals							
Fricatives Unvoiced / Voiced							
Affricates Unvoiced / Voiced							
Glides Unvoiced / Voiced							
Liquids							

Consonant Phonemes by Place and Manner of Articulation

		Lips	Teeth/ Lips	Tongue/ Teeth	Ridge/ Teeth	Roof of Mouth	Back of Throat	Glottis
Stops	Unvoiced	/p/			/t/		/k/	
	Voiced	/b/			/d/		/g/	
Nasals		/m/			/n/		/ng/	
Fricatives	Unvoiced		/f/	/th/	/s/	/sh/		
	Voiced		/v/	/th/	/z/	/zh/		
Affricates	Unvoiced					/ch/		
	Voiced					/j/		
Glides	Unvoiced						/wh/	/h/
	Voiced					/y/	/w/	
Liquids					/l/ /r/			

The stops /b/ and /p/ differ only in the feature called **voicing**. Eight more pairs of consonants on the chart are distinguished from each other only by voicing. One of the pair is voiced, or spoken with the vocal cords engaged. The other of the pair is unvoiced, or spoken with the vocal cords quiet. Everything else about the way the phonemes are pronounced is the same. For this reason, some instructional systems call these pairs "consonant brothers" or "consonant pairs." The difference can be detected if you hold your hands over your ears:

Say /p/ and /b/. Now say /m/.

With the upper teeth on the lower lip, two more consonants can be formed, /f/ and /v/. These differ only in the feature of voicing. You may want to look in a mirror to see that the appearance and position of the mouth does not change when this consonant pair is pronounced.

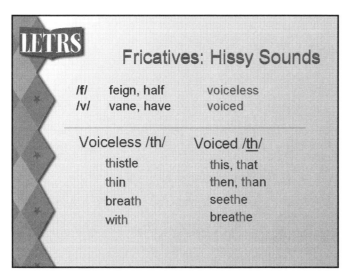

Slide 18

Moving back in the mouth, we make two consonants with the tongue between the teeth. In English, these two consonants are spelled exactly the same way. One of the *th* phonemes is voiced and the other is unvoiced. The unvoiced /th/ begins the words *thick* and *thin* and ends the words *with* and *death*; the voiced /th/ begins the words *this* and *that* and ends the words *bathe* and *writhe*. This distinction is subtle, difficult for many people to hear, and not terribly important because the same digraph is used to spell both phonemes. The phoneme distinction contrasts some word pairs such as *ether* and *either*, *cloth* and *clothe*, *breath* and *breathe*, and *wreath* and *wreathe*. These sounds are called **fricatives** because there is a lot of friction created when the air is forced through small spaces during articulation.

Say /th/, /th/, /f/, and /v/ with clear voicing contrasts.

Middle Mouth Consonants

/t/	teal, mate	voiceless stop
/d/	deal, made	voiced stop
/n/	kneel, mane	nasal
/s/	seal, mace	voiceless fricative
/z/	zeal, maze	voiced fricative

Slide 19

Placing the tongue behind the upper teeth, we can produce five more consonants in English. The stop consonants /t/ and /d/ differ from each other only in voicing. The nasal /n/ shares features with /m/ but the tongue is behind the teeth. The fricative pair /s/ and /z/ also differ only in voicing; the tongue is still behind the teeth. Fricatives are hissy sounds made with a lot of friction when the air is pushed through the mouth. When clusters /nts/ and /mps/ occur at the ends of words such as *elephants* and *jumps*, children feel only one speech gesture—the tongue behind the teeth—and may have trouble differentiating or feeling all of the individual phonemes that the letters represent.

Say /t/, /d/, /n/, /s/, /z/ and feel your tongue position.

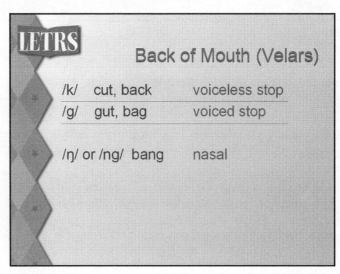

Back of Mouth (Velars)

/k/	cut, back	voiceless stop
/g/	gut, bag	voiced stop
/ŋ/ or /ng/	bang	nasal

Slide 20

We make three more consonants with the tongue raised against the soft palate in the back of the throat: /k/, /g/, and /ng/. In linguistic terminology these are called **velars** because the tongue is raised up against the velum in the back of the throat. The /k/ and /g/ again differ only in voicing. Students quite commonly confuse these phonemes when they occur at the ends of words such as *sack*, *sag*, and *sang*, or *back*, *bag*, and *bang*. Students who write SIG for *sing* may be substituting sounds for one another that are made in the same part of the mouth.

Say /k/, /g/, and /ng/. Feel the tongue.

Affricates and Fricatives

/ch/	pitchin', batch	voiceless affricate
/j/	pigeon, badge	voiced affricate
/sh/	fission, thresher	voiceless fricative
/zh/	vision, treasure	voiced fricative

Slide 21

Another two consonants have the tongue behind the teeth and placed on the hard palate on the roof of the mouth. These **affricates**, /ch/ and /j/, differ only in voicing, as in *cherry* and *Jerry*. They stop the air and then release it.

Say the sounds /ch/ and /j/.

Fricatives, again, are hissy sounds. Another voiced/voiceless pair includes /sh/ and /zh/. These and all fricatives are also continuants; they can be held out or stretched. The phoneme /zh/ does not begin any words of English origin. It is found in words such as *genre* and *entourage* (French), *treasure* (French/Latin), and *azure* (Persian). Many phonics systems do not teach it at all.

Say /sh/ and /zh/. Say *garage* with /zh/.

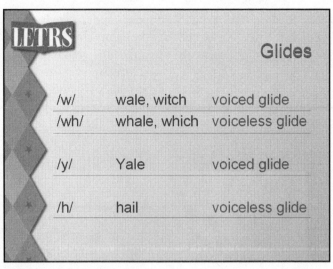

Slide 22

Two groups of consonant phonemes remain to be accounted for: the **glides** and the **liquids**. Glides, along with the liquids, have vowel-like qualities and work with vowels in special ways. They include /w/, /wh/, /y/, and the glottal sound /h/. Glides are consonants that are always followed by a vowel and that literally glide right into it. The consonants /y/ and /w/ are hard to separate from the vowel that follows them.

> Say _yell_ and _well_; say _help_ and _whelp_; say _wile_ and _while_; say _wither_ and _whither_.

The voiceless glide /wh/, which is spelled with a _wh_, is losing its distinctiveness in American speech. Many Americans pronounce the beginning consonants in the words _whether_ and _weather_ the same way, although British speakers tend to retain the distinction between the voiced /w/ and the voiceless /wh/. The distinction is a phonetic fiction we promote to help children remember which words have the _wh_ spelling.

> Why do children confuse _when_ and _went_?

_____

_____

_____

_____

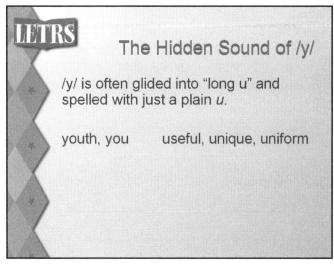

Slide 23

The glide /y/ is often placed in front of the vowel /ū/ (long u). In fact, the words *usual* and *unicorn* begin with the /y/, just like the words *you* and *yule*. Words such as *cute* and *funeral* have a hidden /y/ before the /ū/. This combination is often represented with one letter, *u*, in standard spelling.

Say *ooze* and *use*. Which one has a /y/?

The glottal sound /h/ is formed with the throat open and no other obstruction of the air stream. It is always followed by a vowel. Say, "Harry ran home." We also say "a historical event," not "an historical event" because the /h/ is a consonant and the article "an" is used only before vowels.

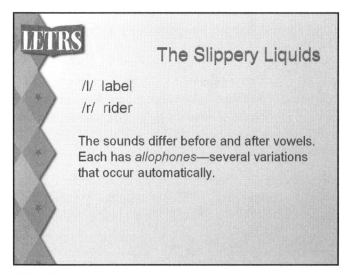

Slide 24

The liquids /l/ and /r/ are slippery phonemes to describe, imitate, produce in isolation, or separate from vowels that precede them. They are aptly named: they seem to float in the mouth. They influence vowels that come before them. Their pronunciation changes somewhat according to the sounds that surround them.

Some languages have no liquids at all. Others, notably Cantonese and Japanese, have one liquid phoneme, pronounced like both /l/ and /r/. Thus, words with liquids may be difficult for speakers of these Asian languages to articulate and they may substitute /l/ for /r/.

Say *scored, scold, scour, scowl.* Feel what the liquids do to the vowels.

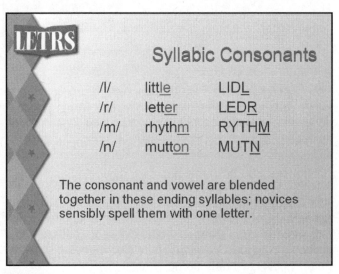

Slide 25

The liquids and nasals, including /l/, /r/, /m/, and /n/, can stand in for whole syllables at the ends of words. In a word such as *mutton*, the last syllable is often pronounced like /n/. The vowel is there but it overlaps with the consonant so much that we do not hear or pronounce a separate vowel segment. In the abstract, there is a vowel in every syllable, but when the vowel is blended with a consonant in words such as *little* (/l/), *rhythm* (/m/), and *better* (/r/), it is hidden. Of course, /m/, /n/, /r/, and /l/ can also be nonsyllabic single consonants as in *need*, *mystery*, *red*, and *laugh*.

Children's early spellings often omit vowel letters from final syllables pronounced like /l/, /r/, /m/, and /n/. The spellings are phonetically accurate because no separate vowel is articulated in these words.

LEDR (letter)   MITN (mitten)   LIDL (little)

Exercise #6: Identify Beginning and Ending Consonants

Identify, say, and write the symbol for the consonant sounds that begin and end each word below. Don't be fooled by the word's spelling!

come _____	bridge _____	seethe _____
knob _____	crave _____	young _____
cage _____	chaise _____	rhyme _____
wrinkle _____	white _____	phone _____
one _____	united _____	gnat _____
thresh _____	hymn _____	psychic _____
queen _____	rouge _____	league _____
giant _____	whole _____	wage _____
rose _____	there _____	south _____

Vowels and Their Articulation

What's a Vowel?

- It's not a consonant.
- It's an open, voiced sound.
- Spoken syllables must have one.
- Written syllables almost always have one (exception *-ism, rhythm*).
- We teach 18 vowels, including three vowel-r combos.

Slide 26

When asked to define a vowel, most teachers will say "a, e, i, o, u, and sometimes y." This answer refers to the number of vowel letters, not the number of vowel phonemes. English has 15 vowel phonemes, plus at least three more vowel-r combinations that are classified by many linguists as vowels. Vowels are absolutely necessary for words, as no syllable can be without a vowel, but vowels are quite variable from dialect to dialect and from geographic region to geographic region.

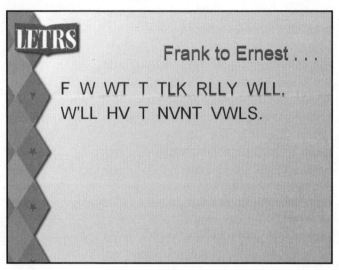

Slide 27

Vowels carry the tune when we sing. It is possible to sing the words to any of your favorite songs by leaving off the consonants and singing the vowels. On the other hand, it would be impossible to sing with only the consonants.

English has many more vowel sounds than Spanish and other Romance languages. The spellings for those vowels are quite variable. It is vowels, both their spoken and written forms, that give students the most trouble. Nevertheless, we will present a system for understanding and teaching vowels according to Standard English. Standard English is represented in dictionaries and grammar books, but most of us actually speak a variation of that abstract standard.

The arrangement of vowels that appears on the chart on page 34 may need to be modified for certain regions of the United States. It can be used to begin a discussion of the vowel pronunciation differences in dialects and other languages.

The Speech Sounds of English: Phonetics, Phonology, and Phoneme Awareness

The Vowels

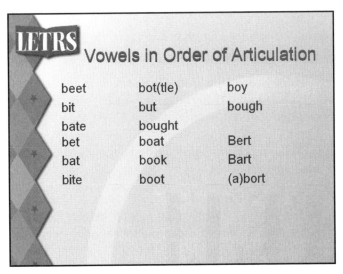

Slide 28

The fifteen English vowels can be distinguished from one another by using the dimensions of tongue position (**front, mid, back**), tongue height (**high to low**), and lip shape (**rounded and unrounded**). Most of the vowels can be contrasted by placing them between the consonants /b/ and /t/ (or a substitute when necessary) and forming a series of words:

beet	bot(tle)	boy
bit	but	bough
bate	bought	
bet	boat	Bert
bat	book	Bart
bite	boot	(a)bort

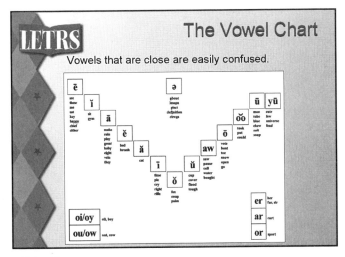

Slide 29

The vowels in the Vowel Chart (page 34) are arranged according their proximity to one another in articulation. Front, high vowels are made with the mouth in a smile position, beginning with /ē/. As the tongue drops step by step and the mouth opens to say each vowel in succession, /ē/, /ĭ/, /ā/, /ĕ/, /ă/, /ī/, the jaw drops to its most open (low, mid) position for /ŏ/, as in the words *father* or *pot*.

The next vowel /ŭ/, as in *stuff* and *stubborn*, is sometimes perceived as being slightly in front of /ŏ/ and slightly higher. It is a low, middle vowel similar to /ŏ/, and is sometimes referred to as the accented cousin of **schwa** [ə], the indistinct vowel that floats in the middle of the mouth. As the four back vowels are spoken in order, the mouth closes slowly: /au/, /ō/, /oo/, /ū/. All four back vowels are made with the lips rounded.

The difference between adjacent vowels on the chart is one small adjustment in closure of the jaw and a small shift of tongue height. Beginning with the highest front vowel, /ē/ as in *beet*, one can say the vowel sequence and watch in a mirror how the mouth changes little by little. All the front vowels are unrounded in English, but the four back vowels are all rounded. (Note that there are front rounded vowels in French, as in *tu* and *vieux*, and in German, as in *Tür* and *Müle*).

Exercise #7: Complete the Blank Chart (page 33) and Say the Vowels

Say the vowels in order, following the leader, until you can try the sequence yourself.

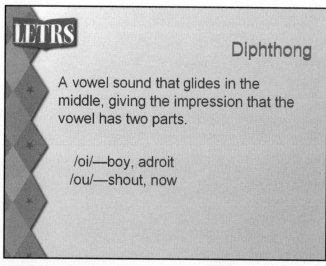

Slide 30

The vowels that do not fit in the step by step sequence are the **diphthongs** /oi/ and /ou/ and **schwa** [ə]. Diphthongs are vowels that glide in the middle. The mouth position shifts during the production of the single vowel phoneme. When you say *boy* notice how the mouth begins with a back, rounded position /au/ and shifts or glides to a front, smiley position, /ē/. It shifts as well with *bow* (as in,

The Speech Sounds of English: Phonetics, Phonology, and Phoneme Awareness

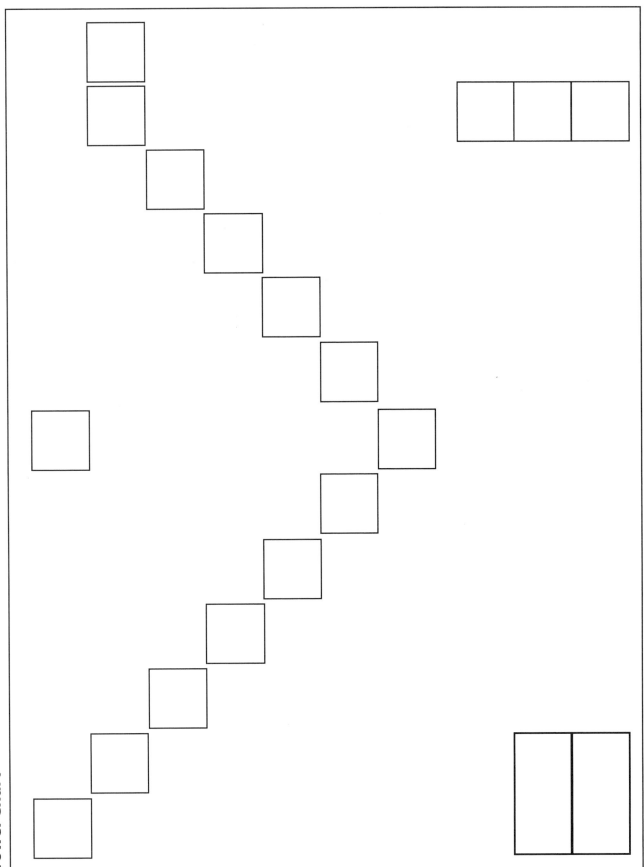

Vowel Chart

Vowel Chart

ē	ĭ	ā	ĕ	ă	ī	ŏ	ĕ	ŭ	aw	ō	ŏŏ	ū	yū
see	sit	make	bed	cat	time	fox	about	cup	saw	vote	took	moo	cute
these	gym	rain	breath		pie	swap	lesson	cover	pause	boat	put	tube	few
me		play			cry	palm	elect	flood	call	toe	could	blue	universe
eat		great			right		definition	tough	water	snow		chew	feud
key		baby			rifle		circus		bought	open		suit	
happy		eight								go		soup	
chief		vein											
either		they											

er	her, fur, sir
ar	cart
or	sport

oi/oy	oil, boy
ou/ow	out, cow

take a *bow* after a performance) from a front position /ă/ to a lip-rounded position /ū/. A third diphthong, /ī/, is placed on the main Vowel Chart because of its relationship to /ŏ/. Children often judge that these vowels are neighbors; thus, they might mistake *light* for *lot* in spelling. The mouth also shifts or glides at the end of the vowel as in *pie*. It is important, however, to realize that the glide is a property of the vowel phoneme /ī/, not a separate vowel. Each diphthong is one vowel phoneme.

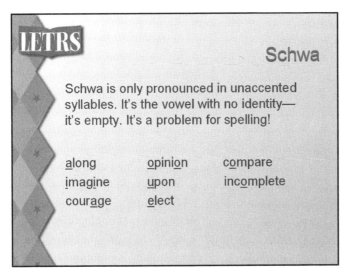

Slide 31

Schwa [ə] is a mid, central, indistinct vowel. In English the vowel in an unstressed syllable often "reduces" to schwa. For example, the root word *commerce* has an /ŏ/ in the first syllable, but its derivation *commercial* reduces that first vowel to schwa when the stress shifts to the second syllable. Schwa reduction presents a problem for children learning to spell because they must learn the identity of vowels based on other, related words or by memorization. Schwa can be spelled with any of the vowel letters in standard orthography (*alone, effect, definition, commence, upon*).

Sometimes the schwa sounds more like an /ĭ/ than an /ŭ/, as in *surface*. One way to recognize a schwa is that it cannot easily be "sounded out" in spelling. The mid-low vowel /ŭ/ sounds like an "accented schwa" but it is found in stressed syllables only, as in *but, butter*, and *supper* and is usually spelled with "short u."

The terms **long** and **short** are in the terminology of phonics instruction but do not mean the same thing in phonetics. The terms, although traditional among educators, do not correspond to how long a vowel is held out when spoken; a "long" vowel is not longer than a "short" vowel. The linguistic terms **tense** and

lax refer to the muscle strength involved in producing the vowels and are used instead of *long* and *short* by linguists. The third category of vowels is diphthongs. Here are the three main groupings:

Long	Short	Diphthong
beet	bit	(bite)
bait	bet	boil
boat	bat	bout
boot	pot	
(bite)	but	
	bought	
	book	

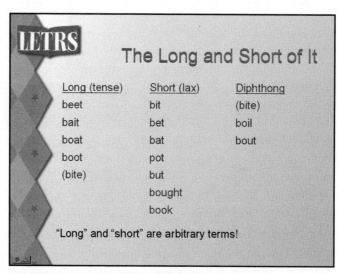

Slide 32

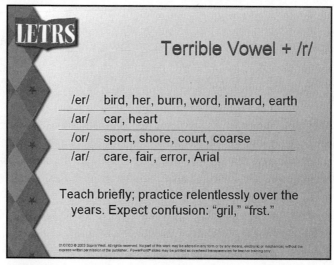

Slide 33

When vowels are followed by /r/, they often change their identity. They may become totally combined with /r/ as in /er/, which is one indivisible phoneme. They may be slightly separated from /r/ but changed by /r/, as in /ar/ and /or/. Or they may keep their original sound, as in /ār/ (fair), /ēr/ (fear), and /īr/ (fire). The spellings for these sounds are variable and difficult for children to learn. Furthermore, many children with speech problems or phonological processing weaknesses substitute phonemes for /r/ or have trouble pronouncing the sound. Blends with /r/, such as *cr*, *sr*, *tr* are hard for many children to spell.

Exercise #8: Place Words on the Vowel Chart

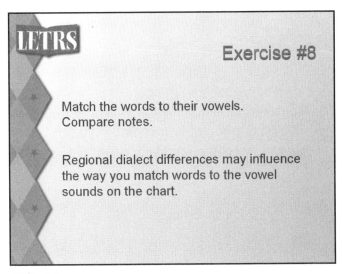

Slide 34

Identify the vowel sounds in the following words by writing them next to the matching vowel on the Vowel Chart on page 33. Dialect may influence your choices.

Words:	chew	heard	staff	vein	blythe	
	hearth	chief	thou	calm	dove	scald
	dread	choice	hymn	could	pour	most

Which vowel is not represented?

Compare notes with others. Which vowels are the most variable in regional dialects?

Exercise #9: Model Segmenting by Phoneme

Exercise #9: Segment Words

2	3	4	5
zoo	mouse	post	stamp
shoe	cheese	jump	shrink
dough	song	grab	plates

Slide 35

1. Given the following words, practice segmenting each one into its component phonemes. Say the word first; then say each sound as you move a penny, chip, or block into a square. Then, slide your finger under the whole word as you blend it back together. Get ready to model for the group.

(2) zoo, shoe, dough

(4) post, jump, grab

(3) mouse, cheese, song

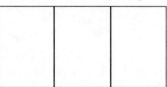

(5) stamp, shrink, plates

2. Now, add five words to each list. Get ready to demonstrate segmentation of these words.

Chameleon Phonemes: How Phonemes Change in Speech

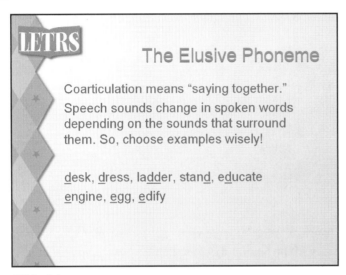

Slide 36

Children must be able to identify the speech sounds in words in order to match symbols to those sounds in reading and spelling. If teaching children to be aware of phonemes in words were as simple as listing them and pronouncing them, however, instruction would be very straightforward. Unfortunately, phonemes are elusive; they change when they are put into words, and some are difficult to pronounce out of the context of a whole word.

Phonemes in words are **coarticulated**, meaning they are spoken together as a seamless unit. There are no spaces between the phonemes in words such as /g/ /oo/ /d/ /m/ /or/ /n/ /i/ /ng/. As a consequence, the features of phonemes spread from one to the other, like unfixed dye in fabric. In the process, phonemes are slightly changed. The results are called **allophones**—several variations of the same phoneme that occur automatically, such as the different /ĕ/ sounds in these words:

engine: the /ĕ/ is nasalized before /n/

egg: the /ĕ/ is raised toward the /ā/ sound

edify: the /ĕ/ is closest to its "standard" form

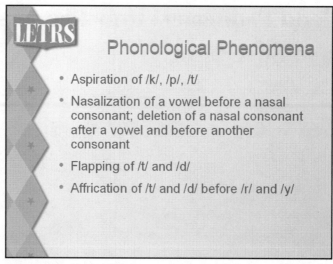

Slide 37

Aspiration. The voiceless stop consonants, /k/, /p/, and /t/, are pronounced with a push of breath in the beginnings of syllables, before vowels, and if they are the first sound in a consonant blend.

If /k/, /p/, or /t/ are the second sound in a blend, as in *skin*, *spun*, or *stem*, they are **unaspirated**. There is no push of breath. Children are more likely to mistake them for their voiced brothers, /g/, /b/, and /d/ when they are unaspirated. Thus, children may make these spelling substitutions:

SGIN/skin	SGARY/scary
SBYDR/spider	SBESL/special
SDASHN/station	SDRT/start

Final consonants /k/, /t/, and /p/ are also unaspirated and are more often confused with their voiced counterparts or omitted altogether in speech or spelling.

Nasalization. Every vowel that occurs before a nasal consonant, /m/, /n/, or /ng/, becomes **nasalized**. That is, the vowel sound itself gets pushed through the nose, in anticipation of the nasal consonant that follows it. Say these word pairs, while holding your nose:

bad, band

said, send

rat, rant

dote, don't

sick, sink

puck, punk

The reason that the final blends *nt*, *mp*, and *nk* are hard for children to spell is that the nasal sound gets "lost" in articulation. The nasal feature of the consonant bleeds into the vowel; the vowel takes on the nasality of the consonant /m/, /n/, or /ng/ in anticipation of the consonant. The nasal consonant is articulated with a tongue gesture similar to the consonant that follows it, and it becomes part of one speech gesture. It can't be felt as a separate segment. Thus, children commonly misspell words such as:

SIK/sink

BASEMET/basement

JUPPY/jumpy

SIPLE/simple

Many children will tune into the presence of the nasal sound if they are asked to hold their nose during the pronunciation of words with /m/, /n/, or /ng/.

Flapping. British speakers of English sometimes deride American English speech as lazy or sloppy. However, the sins of American speech are committed by all of us because they are rule-based; we speak the way we do because of dialect characteristics, not character lapses. One of the automatic, rule-based changes that American speakers make more than British speakers is to change the middle /t/ to a tongue flap that sounds like /d/ when it is between an accented and unaccented vowel such as:

water   better   writer   British   little

This speech habit of changing the middle /t/ to a tongue flap, called **flapping**, explains why children make sensible spelling attempts such as WADR, LIDL, BEDR, BUDR, and BRIDISH. The middle /d/ in words such as *rider*, *ladle*, and *skidding* is also reduced to a tongue flap. It is not pronounced the same way as the /d/ in *desk*.

Affrication of /t/ and /d/. Teachers of kindergarteners and first graders may have noticed the tendency of young children to spell this way:

CHRAN/train   JRS/dress

CHRICK/trick   JRAGIN/dragon

HRET/treat   GRAN/drain

NACHR/nature   EJUKATE/educate

When we pronounce a /t/ or /d/ before an /r/ or a /y/, each consonant becomes affricated. That is, in anticipation of the /r/, our mouths pucker up and the phonemes are very close to /ch/ and /j/. Children may use the letter *h* to spell this sound because the *h* is the only letter name that has the /ch/ sound in it. Likewise they may use either *j* or *g* to spell the /j/ sound.

Exercise #10: Analyze Children's Writing

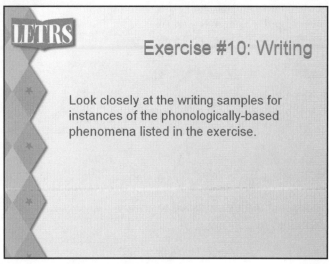

Slide 38

Look at these examples of children's writing. These children are spelling some words by sound, others by established sight word habits, and others by copying from a chart.

Identify the words that show:

1. Affrication of /t/ or /d/ so that it is changed to /ch/ or /j/.

2. Flapping of a medial /t/ so that it is changed to /d/.

3. Voiced/voiceless consonant substitution, or other substitution of consonants pronounced similarly.

4. Trouble with a consonant cluster (blend).

5. Substitution of vowels that are similar in articulation.

6. Omission of a nasal consonant after a vowel and before a consonant, or omission of /r/ or /l/ after a vowel.

7. Use of a single letter for a syllabic consonant /l/, /m/, or /r/.

8. Use of letter names to stand for specific phonemes (s, r).

9. Omission or confusion of inflected endings (e.g., -ed, -s, -ing).

10. Alternative letter possibility (silent e).

(continued) **Exercise #10:** Analyze Children's Writing

Sometime you can make pancakes with agg and with mike and you can make pancakes with buttr and grise.

—End of second grade

_____

_____

_____

I was also frighten when i was going home and i was by lots of trees and it was lighting. I was so frightened my that. Sometime thing could be so frightened that you could junp out of your shoes. Things that are frightingly can scare you that you will not no what happen to you. I hate frighened things.

—End of fourth grade

_____

_____

_____

I went to the brthday. Me and Cassd made are bedroom into a hotid home. I shod my grem and grap.

—Beginning of first grade

_____

_____

_____

(continued) **Exercise #10:** Analyze Children's Writing

transplant, strongest, unbleded, quitet, anything, slender.
—Fourth grade spelling test result

I am gini bee a devil for halawene. I am going tric treding for Halawene. I fed the sdrae [stray] cat uesterday.
—Beginning of first grade

Then the witch came off her broomstc. Then the witch went ovr the gobrigh [drawbridge]. Than the witch noct on the door then the princess opind the door then the witch grab the princess and then the witct jragd that princess to her hows. Then a prince so the witch jragen the princss to her hows. Then the prince went aftr the witch bat the prince was to fat. Then the naxt dai the witch jragd the princss to a hi op towr with no stars no dor.
—May of kindergarten*

---

* Child who had been taught through very systematic phonetic system, "Focus on Phonemes," by Jan Crosby and Pat Tyborowski (for more information, call 508-753-7551 or go to the website www.thephonicsformula.com). The first three samples on the following page are also from children in that class.

(continued) **Exercise #10:** Analyze Children's Writing

A capl uers [years] latr. The king did [died] then a witch came riden ovr the casl.

—Kindergarten

_____

_____

_____

Once upon a time there was a princess and a prince and a jagin. The dragin poot the princess in a kaj. The prince rextyoud [rescued] the princess and livd hapulee evr after.

—Kindergarten

_____

_____

_____

I am going to florlda and i will bring my bathing sut and a short sleve shrt and shorts. When i get there i will go and see micee mous and minee mous and then i will go to the bech.

—Kindergarten

_____

_____

_____

_____

_____

_____

_____

Apirl hand lenkin worked at the white house

—End of kindergarten; (child lives in Washington, D.C.)

_____

_____

_____

_____

Spanish Phonology

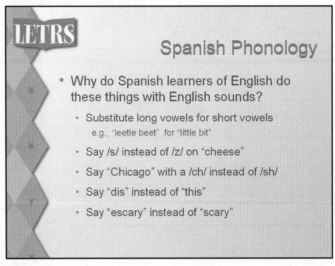

Slide 39

Spanish Vowels

In Spanish, there are fewer phonemes (22) than in English (40+). The greatest difference between these language systems is the number of vowels (five vs. eighteen). The five Spanish vowels are easy to distinguish from one another, like the long vowels in English, and are represented with consistent spellings. In Spanish reading instruction, children are usually taught the vowel correspondences first. They are as follows:

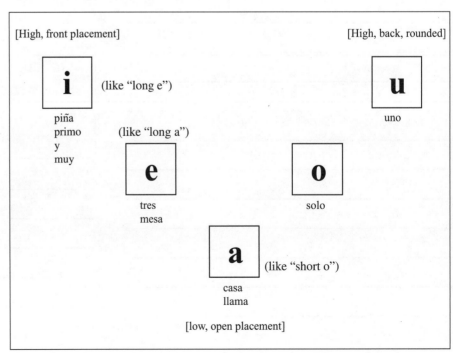

Two or three vowels often occur in sequence. Each retains its identity. In some words, two adjacent vowels belong to different syllables: *fiesta, Diablo, lea.*

In some words, the adjacent vowels occur within the same syllable and are glided into one vowel sound: *cielo, muy, voy, puede.*

Trigraphs are three vowels sequenced within one syllable, or one vowel phoneme with three parts: *buey, guia.*

Spanish Consonants

Bilabial (two lips)	Labio-Dental (teeth and lips)	Alveolar (tongue behind teeth)	Palatal	Velar	Glottal
/p/ (pera)		/t/ (taza)		/k/ (que) (casa)	
/b/ (bueno) (vaca)		/d/ (dos)		/g/ (gato)	
/m/ (mano)		/n/ (nido)	/ñ/ (año)		
	/f/ (fiesta)	/s/ (silla) (zapato)	/ch/ (Chicano)		/x/ (Mexico)
			/y/ (llama) (yo)		/h/ (jicama)
		/l/ (limon)			
		/r/ (rio) (barro)			

With seventeen consonants and five vowels, Spanish has only twenty-two phonemes—almost half of the number of English phonemes. The twenty-nine symbols used to represent those sounds have a much more consistent correspondence pattern than English. As with English speakers, Spanish children need practice identifying, segmenting, and blending phonemes; the patterns to be practiced, however, are usually open syllables that end with a vowel.

Phonological Patterns of Hispanic Learners of English

Spanish speakers who are learning English are likely to make these substitutions:

- ◆ /ch/ for /sh/
- ◆ /s/ for /z/
- ◆ /t/ or /d/ for /th/
- ◆ /es/ for /s/ at the beginning of words
- ◆ reduction of word-final consonant clusters

Understanding Dialect Differences

What Is Dialect?

Dialects[7] are versions of the same language spoken by groups of people who are separated socially or geographically. The speakers of different dialects understand each other because they share the same basic language system, but their speech varies systematically or predictably in phonology, word use, or grammar. **Dialect interference** in a school setting occurs if the phonology or usage of a student's dialect differs substantially from the dialect spoken by the teacher. Dialect interference can also occur if the student's dialect is substantially different from the Standard English forms in written text.

Consider these differences between British English and American English words for the same thing:

> lift – elevator
>
> petrol – gasoline
>
> public school – private school
>
> trousers – pants
>
> pint – mug of beer

Ways of pronouncing words differ in various regions of the United States. In specific regions, words are confusable because they are pronounced the same way, as follows:

> Boston: farther, father (drop the /r/)
>
> Washington: warsh, wash (insert /r/)
>
> Tennessee: oil, all
>
> Texas: pin, pen
>
> Southern California: cot, caught

[7] More information on dialect is available in Fromkin and Rodman, 1998.

Children benefit from systematic comparisons between the more formal or Standard English used in print and their oral language, especially during writing instruction. The goal of such comparisons is not to change the way students speak, but to help them become conscious of words, to check spelling and writing, and to choose words according to what the situational context calls for. For example, we usually modify our speech to a more formal style when we are in the presence of authorities, but change to a nurturing style when we are in the presence of young children. Writing demands certain forms that speaking does not.

Phonological Patterns of AAVE

Linguists and community members have debated whether African American vernacular English (AAVE) is a dialect of Standard English or a language system deserving of its own name, Ebonics. No matter which perspective one embraces, AAVE has predictable and known phonological, syntactical, pragmatic, and semantic differences from Standard English. Many of these differences can be traced back to the African languages spoken by slaves shipped to this country in the seventeenth, eighteenth, and nineteenth centuries, and the influence of the southern English dialect of the slave-holders. Some common dialect features of AAVE are:

◆ Reduction or simplification of consonant blends at the ends of words, when the blend includes two unvoiced or two voiced consonants.

toas'   tes'   fac'   kep'   des'
toast   test   fact   kept   desk

◆ Omission or confusion of inflections *-ed*, *-ing*, and *-s*; this is related to the consonant cluster reduction principle.

Sometime thing could be so frightened that you could jump out of your shoes.

◆ Simplification of third person singular verb. Also, the word *agg* (below) represents both a vowel spelling that pairs a long vowel with the closest short vowel but that also leaves off the plural.

He like to make pancake with agg.

◆ Initial /th/ pronounced /d/ (*dis* for *this*); medial /th/ pronounced /v/ (*brover* for *brother*); and final /th/ pronounced /f/ (*bof* for *both*). (African languages had no /th/ sound.)

◆ Omission of the verb "to be," or using "be" to indicate an action of continuing duration.

He be waiting on you every single day!
He waiting downstairs; hurry up!

♦ Changing *ask* to *aks*. Only this word is affected, as the consonant reversal does not occur in words such as *masking* or *skin*.

♦ Deleting or softening /l/ and /r/ after vowels. This is common to many southern American dialects, which in turn were related to southern British dialects.

Dat's a po' o'd dog.

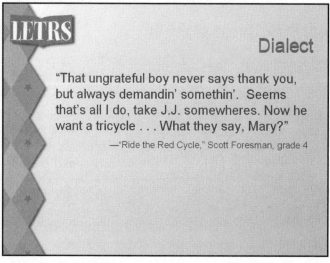

Slide 40

There are many more differences between AAVE, Standard American English, and other regional and social dialects in our country, but these few examples should suffice to illustrate the predictable, rule-based characteristics that distinguish one form of speech from another. No dialect is inferior. A constructive teacher identifies, illustrates, and teaches important Standard English differences necessary for comprehending, speaking, reading, and writing using a neutral and factual approach.

Teaching Phonological Skill: Some Specifics

Sound Blending

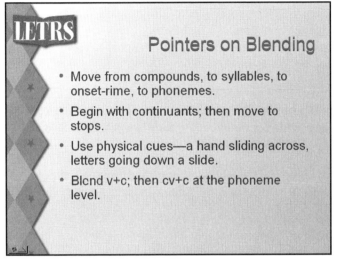

Slide 41

Sound **blending** exercises begin with blending syllables and compound parts into words, progress to blending onsets and rimes, and gradually lead to sound by sound blending of two- and three-phoneme words. A few words with more than three speech sounds may be used with kindergarten children who are progressing well.

The earliest oral blending exercises use words that begin with **continuous** consonants, not stops. Thus, /m/, /n/, /sh/, /th/, /f/, /v/, /s/, /z/, /sh/, /l/, and /r/ can be blended more easily than /b/, /p/, /d/, /t/, /g/, /k/, /j/, or /ch/. All the continuant consonants and vowels can be "sung" together to support blending. For example, the sounds /v/ /a/ /n/ can be held out to exaggerate their identity.

◆ Start with vowel-consonant combinations (*up, eat, at, it, ooze, edge*).

◆ Model; help; let the student do one alone.

◆ Move to consonant-vowel-consonant combinations that begin with continuant sounds.

◆ Use pictures of target words to help the student identify the word.

◆ Move chips or letter tiles from left to right as sounds are blended. Show them sliding together down a slide.

◆ Blend the first two sounds together, and then have the student add the last sound. Have the student change the last sound to make a new word.

- Have the student touch each tile or letter while saying each sound, then go back and slide the student's finger across as the sounds are blended with the teacher's help.

Sound Segmentation

Oral phoneme segmentation exercises help children to separate words into sounds. Exercises should follow the progression of difficulty. Children's phonetic (temporary) spellings show how well they are "hearing" the sounds in words. Children will have trouble spelling unless they can separate and identify the sounds that the letters represent.

Oral blending and oral segmentation tasks should receive emphasis because they are most closely connected to early reading and writing development. They can be taught along with activities for speech sound identification, comparison, substitution, and deletion.

Wide phoneme contrasts, such as "long e" and "long o," should precede closer contrasts among the vowels and consonants, such as /ĭ/ and /ĕ/, or /f/ and /v/.

Exercise #11: Minimal Pairs

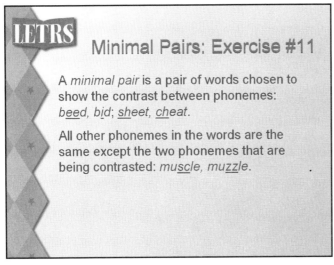

Slide 42

Generate minimally contrasting pairs of words. A **minimal pair** differs only in one speech sound. Deliberate use of these pairs in phonological awareness activities heightens children's sensitivity to subtle differences among words. Practice distinguishing minimally contrasting pairs also helps children hear sounds in English that may not be present in their first language.

Think of words in which every phoneme is the same except for the target phoneme pair. Try to think of pairs that differ in the beginning sounds, ending sounds, and even medial sounds. An example of each is given.

/ē/, /ĭ/ (beed, bid)   /ā/, /ĕ/ (fail, fell)   /ĭ/, /ĕ/ (pin, pen)

_____   _____   _____

/ŭ/, /ŏ/ (bud, bod)   /ŏ/, /aw/ (cot, caught)   /ow/, /oy/ (plow, ploy)

_____   _____   _____

/ch/, /j/ (rich, ridge)   /f/, /v/ (half, have)   /l/, /r/ (lock, rock)

_____   _____   _____

/y/, /w/ (yell, well)

_____

Exercise #12: Tasks for Role Play and Practice

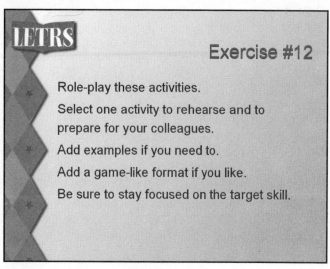

Slide 43

Preschool or Beginning Kindergarten Level

1. Read books aloud with rhyme patterns and alliteration. Let children chime in and supply the rhyme or extend the alliteration.

2. Rhyme Judgement:
   "Words rhyme if the last part of each word sounds the same. *Cake* and *bake* rhyme; so do *merry* and *cherry*. Listen while I say the poem, and get ready to say the rhyming word. Jack and *Jill* went up the *hill*. What words rhyme?"

3. Rhyme Production:
   "Let's play a game. I'll say three words that rhyme—that sound alike on the end. You say one more word that rhymes. It can be a silly word. Hinky, pinky, slinky, _____. Say a word that sounds like (rhymes with) *star*."

4. Rhyme Matching:
   "Listen carefully. Rhyming Robot wants to find a match for each of his favorite words. If one of his favorite words is *shake*, which of these words can he have? Meat, *steak*, corn."

5. Alliteration:
   "Peter Piper picked a peck of pickled peppers."
   "Let's make a silly sentence with /n/ words. Neat Nancy . . ."

(continued) **Exercise #12:** Tasks for Role Play and Practice

6. Syllable Blending:

"Silly Cesar speaks very slowly. What word is Silly Cesar saying?"

ta-ble	hos-pi-tal	tan-ger-ine
roll-er-blades	fire-truck	play-ground

7. Syllable Deletion:

"Let's play a game with words. We're going to break some long words into parts and leave a part out. If I say *toothpaste*, and then leave off the *tooth*, what's left? That's right, *paste*. Let's try some more."

What's *baseball* without *ball*? What's *butterfly* without *butter*?
What's *paddleboat* without *boat*? What's *Sunday* without *day*?
What's *power* without *er*? What's *telephone* without *tele*?

8. Syllable counting:

"Inside this treasure chest are lots of things with names that you know. When it's your turn, reach in and take something out. Then clap the syllables as you say the word."
[*Balloon, cricket, calculator, eraser, sharpener, stapler, candlestick, napkin*]

9. Initial sound matching:

"Let's see whose name starts with the same sound as someone else's name. They can stand together. Tanya and Timmy. What sound begins each of your names? Let's think of another name that starts with /t/."

10. Onset-rime division:

"Let's say some words in parts. I'll say the whole word. Then you say the whole word and divide it into two parts. Turn your hand over for each part, like this [model]. C-ar; sh-ip; w-ave; p-ie; sk-ate; d-esk."

More Difficult PA Tasks

11. Final sound matching:

"Listen while I say two words. If they end with the same last sound, repeat the sound."

moon, pen /n/	bridge, page /j/	wish, mash /sh/	brick, steak /k/

(continued) **Exercise #12:** Tasks for Role Play and Practice

12. Say it and move it (phoneme segmentation):

    "Listen to this word: *chick*. Say the word sound by sound while you move the counters in the boxes. Watch me first (/ch/ /i/ /k/). Now you do it. Good. Which one is /k/? Which one is /i/?"

    "Let's try some silly words (nonsense words)."

    pem   zer   uff   zone   cheed

13. Blending phonemes:

    "When I call your name, you can stand up. I'm going to say your name sound by sound: /k/ /r/ /i/ /s/   /h/ /u/ /g/ /o/   /w/ /a/ /n/ /d/ /a/."

14. Initial and final sound substitution:

    "Let's see if we can make some new words by changing just one sound. If I change the /b/ in *bench* to /r/, what new word would I have? If I change the /w/ in *wag* to /t/, what new word do I have? If I change the /l/ in *shell* to /f/, what new word do I have?"

    poodle–noodle   witch–win   race–rays

15. Middle vowel substitution:

    [First, move same-colored chips to show the segmentation of the word. As the vowel is changed, show which chip is changing.]

    "Now we'll make some new words by changing just one sound in the middle—the vowel sound. Here is *moose* (/m/ /ū/ /s/). Let's change *moose* to *mouse*. Which sound is changed? Only the middle one right here—the vowel sound."

    moon–man   fawn–fin   soup–sap   boot–beet

16. Tracking single phoneme changes with colored blocks:

    Give students five blocks or chips with four different colors and one double. Different sounds are represented with different colored blocks, but blocks may represent any sound. Say a word with 1–4 phonemes. Have students show how many sounds are in the word using the blocks. For example, you might start with *day*—two blocks of different colors. Then add, change, delete, or switch the order of one sound at a time. If you change *day* to *date*, the students should add a third block of a different color.

The Speech Sounds of English: Phonetics, Phonology, and Phoneme Awareness

(continued) **Exercise #12:** Tasks for Role Play and Practice

This is also called "chaining" words. Sometimes nonsense words or syllables are used in transitions.

day, date, dot, pot, spot, spit, sit, sits
me, mean, men, zen, zin, zip, chip, pitch, titch, stitch
ouch, out, shout, shoot, shoes, use, dues, twos, stews

17. Sound deletion:
Syllable: Say *potato* without the *po*.
Initial sound: Say *peas* without the /p/.
Final sound: Say *sheet* without the /t/.
Initial Blend: Say *stop* without the /s/.
Final blend: Say *wild* without the /d/.

18. Transition to letter-sound correspondence:
During the "Say it and move it (phoneme segmentation)" activity earlier in this exercise, introduce a first set of 6–8 sound tiles, such as /b/, /p/, /m/, /f/, /ee/, /v/, /t/, or /d/. Note that *ee* and other two-letter combinations can be put on one movable tile because they are one sound-spelling unit. Teach the difference between the quiet and noisy sounds that feel very much the same (/p/, /b/; /f/, /v/; /t/, /d/) and the /m/ that goes through the nose. Use a key word on a sound card to help children remember which letter represents which sound. Reinforce associations through memory games. Be sure the child can point to the right symbol for each sound as the sounds are dictated and then use the symbol to build simple words.

Words to make with letter-sound tiles:
beet, deed, meet, peet, feet, feed, fee, vee, bee

Possible order for adding other sound-letter associations:
/s/, /z/, /n/, /a/
/k/, /g/, /ng/, /o/
/sh/, /ch/, /j/, /i/
/l/, /r/, /w/, /y/, /h/, /u/
[don't teach /zh/ or /wh/ until later]

Vowels by order of articulation on the Vowel Chart:
ee, i, a_e, e, a, i_e, o, u, aw, o_e, oo, u_e, ow, oy, er, ar, or

(continued) **Exercise #12:** Tasks for Role Play and Practice

19. Spelling match game:

    Form two teams. A student from one team selects a word from a word bank or deck of cards with words and reads it aloud. [1 point for correct reading]

    The other team spells the word with tiles or written letters. If the word is correct [2 points], the spelling team takes the next turn as reader. If word is not correct, the spelling team gets one more chance to fix the spelling [1 point if corrected].

20. Pig Latin:

    Make a sentence by removing the first consonant from each word, putting the consonant at the end of the word, and adding the vowel *ay* to it. "Ello-hay, y-may, ame-nay, is-ay, teve-say." [Hello, my name is Steve.]

Exercise #13: Examine Your Program

Think about the phonological awareness component of the program you are teaching in your class. Then, answer these questions:

1. Are the activities sequenced according to a developmental continuum? Where is that continuum explained?

2. Is PA a consistent component of the language arts daily lesson?

3. Does each activity have a clear focus on a linguistic unit that is appropriate for that level (word, syllable, onset-rime, phoneme)?

4. Is oral language manipulation clearly distinguished from written symbol manipulation?

5. Is adequate practice provided?

6. Are the examples for the activities well chosen?

7. How will you measure progress with PA?

Exercise #14: View Videotaped Instruction

View videotapes of teachers at work teaching PA. Discuss the following questions, especially with regard to how instruction might be improved.

1. Is the goal of the activity clear?

2. Is the level of difficulty appropriate for the children?

3. Are the examples well chosen?

4. Are speech sounds clearly and accurately produced?

5. Is there sufficient modeling, practice, and independent demonstration of skill?

6. Is there clarity about the differences among speech sound recognition, letter naming, and sound-symbol association?

Summary

Phonological processing is an umbrella term that encompasses many abilities having to do with speech perception, awareness, memory, retrieval, and production. In part, it accounts for human variability in the ease of learning a foreign language, remembering novel words, recalling names and facts, and spelling. Phonological awareness is a metalinguistic proficiency that includes the ability to divide a word into spoken syllables, onset-rime segments, and individual phonemes. Phoneme awareness is the subskill of phonology that is most closely related to reading and spelling. Learning to decode an alphabetic writing system with phonics requires phoneme awareness.

Speech sounds are divided into consonants and vowels. Each speech sound is distinguished by a set of features, such as oral or nasal, stopped or continuous, voiced or unvoiced, and aspirated or unaspirated production. Speech sounds that are similar in place and manner of articulation are the most easily confused. If children are left on their own to figure out the identity of speech sounds in words, they may not be able to detect all the features that distinguish those sounds. Speech sounds are not articulated separately; they are coarticulated when we speak, and thus, many people have some difficulty segmenting those sounds. Direct teaching is important because it enables children to form accurate concepts of speech sounds that will anchor their learning of the writing system.

Consonants are closed sounds. Vowels are open sounds and are needed in every word and syllable. Identifying the existence of the speech sound inventory is not an easy or obvious task, because the sounds we think of as phonemes are buried in the continuous stream of speech that makes words, phrases, and sentences.

Consonants can be further categorized as stops, nasals, fricatives, affricates, glides, and liquids. There are nine pairs of voiced and unvoiced consonants that are otherwise articulated similarly.

English spelling is a less than optimal system for representing speech sounds. It has too few symbols (twenty-six) for the twenty-five consonants and eighteen vowels. The six vowel letters are overworked in our writing system.

Vowels form the nucleus of a syllable. They are classified on the dimensions of front, mid and back, and high to low. The front vowels are unrounded but the back vowels are made with a rounding of the lips. Vowels may be long (tense), short (lax), or diphthongs. Vowels followed by /r/ have special properties.

Spanish has about half as many phonemes as English and only five vowels, which are spelled consistently. African American vernacular English (AAVE) is characterized by regular phonological changes. Knowing these language differences helps teachers decide what contrasts among words to highlight when Standard English is being taught during language arts.

Instruction in phonological awareness increases the likelihood that children will learn to read and spell. It is essential for children who show signs of early difficulty with sound identification. The PA component of reading and spelling instruction should be explicit, systematic, and informed by an understanding of the developmental progression of PA.

Bibliography

Adams, M., Foorman, B. F., Lundberg, I., & Beeler, T. (1997). *Phonemic awareness in young children: A classroom curriculum*. Baltimore: Paul Brookes Publishing.

Blachman, B., Ball, E. W., Black, R., & Tangel, D. (1999). *Road to the code: A phonological awareness program for young children*. Baltimore: Paul Brookes Publishing.

Blevins, W. (1997). *Phonemic awareness activities for early reading success*. New York: Scholastic.

Brady, S. A. (1997). Ability to encode phonological representations: An underlying difficulty of poor readers. In B. Blachman (Ed.), *Foundations of Reading Acquisition and Dyslexia*. Mahwah, NJ: Lawrence Erlbaum.

Byrne, B., & Fielding-Barnsley, R. (1991). *Sound foundations*. Artarmon, New South Wales, Australia: Leyden Educational Publishers.

Catts, H. (1997). *Sounds abound*. N.p.: LinguiSystems.

Goswami, U. (2000). Phonological and lexical processes. In M. L. Kamil, P. B. Mosenthal, P. D. Pearson, & R. Barr (Eds.), *Handbook of reading research*. Mahwah, NJ: Lawrence Erlbaum Associates.

Greene, J. (2000). *Sounds and letters for reading and spelling*. Longmont, CO: Sopris West Educational Services.

Kingsolver, B. (1999). *The Poisonwood Bible*. New York: HarperCollins.

Lederer, R. (1987). *Anguished English*. Charleston: Wyrick & Co.

Lindamood, P., & Lindamood, C. (N.d.). *The Lindamood phoneme sequencing program for reading, spelling, and speech* (LIPS). Austin, TX: Pro-Ed.

National Reading Panel. (2000). *Report of the National Reading Panel: Teaching Children to Read, An Evidence-Based Assessment of the Scientific Research Literature on Reading and Its Implications for Reading Instruction*. Washington, DC: National Institute of Child Health and Human Development.

Nelson, R.J., Cooper, P., & Gonzalez, J. (2004). *Stepping Stones to Literacy*. Longmont, CO: Sopris West Educational Services.

O'Connor, R., Notari-Syverson, A., & Vadasy, P. F. (1998). *Ladders to literacy: A kindergarten activity book*. Baltimore: Paul Brookes Publishing.

Rath, L. (2001). Phonemic awareness. In S. Brody (Ed.), *Teaching Reading: Language, Letters, and Thought*. Milford, NH: LARC Publishing.

Torgesen, J. K., & Bryant, B. R. (1994). *Phonological awareness training for reading*. Austin, Texas: Pro-Ed.

Tyborowski, P., & Crosby, J. (2001). *Focus on /F/onemes: The complete phonemic awareness curriculum*. Worcester, MA: /F/onemes to Phonics.

Vadasy, P.F., Wayne, S.K., O'Connor, R.E., Jenkins, J.R., Pool, K. Firebaugh, M., & Peyton, J.A. (in press). [Sound Partners]. Working title. Longmont, CO: Sopris West Educational Services.

Suggested Reading

The following are graduate level textbooks often used in beginning linguistics classes that include comprehensive treatments of topics such as phonetics, phonology, morphology, and language processing.

Akmajian, A., Demers, R. A., Farmer, A. K., & Harnish, R. M. (1995). *Linguistics: An introduction to language and communication.* Cambridge, MA: MIT Press.

Edwards, H. T. (1992). *Applied phonetics: The sounds of American English.* San Diego: Singular Publishing Group.

Fromkin, V., & Rodman, R. (1998). *An introduction to language,* 6th Edition. Fort Worth: Harcourt Brace College Publishers.

Ladefoged, P. (1993). *A course in phonetics,* 3rd Edition. Fort Worth: Harcourt Brace Jovanovich.

These journal articles, books, and book chapters are often-cited sources for the empirical findings that support direct instruction of phonological skills for young children and dyslexic children learning to read.

Blachman, B. (1997). *Foundations of reading acquisition and dyslexia.* Mahwah, NJ: Erlbaum.

Bryant, P., MacLean, M., Bradley, L., & Crossland, J. (1990). Rhyme, alliteration, phoneme detection and learning to read. *Developmental Psychology, 26,* 429–438.

Catts, H. (1993). The relationship between speech-language impairments and reading disabilities. *Journal of Speech and Hearing Research, 36,* 948–958.

Elkonin, D. B. (1983). The psychology of mastering the elements of reading. In Simon, B., & Simon, J. (Eds.), *Educational psychology in the USSR.* Standford, CA: Stanford University Press.

Gillon, G.T. (2004). *Phonological awareness: From research to practice.* New York: Guilford Publications.

Liberman, I. Y., Shankweiler, D., & Liberman, A. (1989). The alphabetic principle and learning to read. In Shankweiler, D., & Liberman, I. Y. (Eds.). *Phonology and reading disability: Solving the reading puzzle.* Ann Arbor, MI: University of Michigan Press.

Lundberg, I., Frost, J., & Peterson, O. (1988). Effects of an extensive program for stimulating phonological awareness in preschool children. *Reading Research Quarterly, 23,* 263–284.

Rosner, J. (1971). The Auditory Analysis Test: An initial report. *Journal of Learning Disabilities, 4* (7), 40–48.

Tunmer, W. E., & Hoover, W. A. (1993). Phonological recoding skill and beginning reading. *Reading and Writing: An Interdisciplinary Journal, 5,* 161–179.

Wagner, R. K., Torgesen, J. K., Rashotte, C. A., Hecht, S. A., Barker, T. A., Burgess, S., Donahue, J., & Garon, T. (1997). Changing causal relations between phonological processing abilities and word-level reading as children develop from beginning to fluent readers: A five-year longitudinal study. *Developmental Psychology, 33,* 468–479.

Language Essentials
for Teachers of
Reading and
Spelling

Glossary

Advanced concepts are indicated with an asterisk (*).

*AAVE: African American vernacular English, also called Ebonics or Black English; a dialect with phonological, semantic, and syntactic features that originated with the African languages brought to the Americas by slaves

affix: a morpheme or a meaningful part of a word that is attached before or after a root to modify its meaning; a category that includes prefixes, suffixes, and infixes

*affricate: a speech sound with features of both a fricative and a stop; in English, /ch/ and /j/ are affricates

*affrication: the pronunciation of /t/ as /ch/ in words such as nature, and /d/ as /j/ in words such as educate

alphabetic principle: the principle that letters are used to represent individual phonemes in the spoken word; a critical insight for beginning reading and spelling

alphabetic writing system: a system of symbols that represent each consonant and vowel sound in a language

Anglo-Saxon: Old English, a Germanic language spoken in Britain before the invasion of the Norman French in 1066

base word: a free morpheme, usually of Anglo-Saxon origin, to which affixes can be added

*bound morpheme: a meaningful part of a word that makes words only in combination with other morphemes; includes inflections, roots, prefixes, and derivational suffixes

chunk: a group of letters, processed as a unit, that corresponds to a piece of a word, usually a consonant cluster, rime pattern, syllable, or morpheme

closed sound: a consonant sound made by using the tongue, teeth, or lips to obstruct the air as it is pushed through the vocal cavity

closed syllable: a written syllable containing a single vowel letter that ends in one or more consonants; the vowel sound is short

cluster: adjacent consonants that appear before or after a vowel; a consonant blend

*coarticulation: speaking phonemes together so that the features of each spreads to neighboring phonemes and all the segments are joined into one linguistic unit (a syllable)

concept: an idea that links other facts, words, and ideas together into a coherent whole

consonant: a phoneme (speech sound) that is not a vowel and that is formed by obstructing the flow of air with the teeth, lips, or tongue; also called a closed sound in some instructional programs; English has 25 consonant phonemes

consonant cluster: see cluster

consonant digraph: a two-letter combination that represents one speech sound that is not represented by either letter alone

consonant-le syllable: a written syllable found at the ends of words such as dawdle, single, and rubble

context: the language that surrounds a given word or phrase (linguistic context), or the field of meaningful associations that surrounds a given word or phrase (experiential context)

context processor: the neural networks that bring background knowledge and discourse to bear as word meanings are processed

cumulative instruction: teaching that proceeds in additive steps, building on what was previously taught

decodable text: text in which a high proportion of words (70 to 90%) comprise sound-symbol relationships that have already been taught; used to provide practice with specific decoding skills; a bridge between learning phonics and the application of phonics in independent reading of text

decoding: the ability to translate a word from print to speech, usually by employing knowledge of sound-symbol correspondences; also the act of deciphering a new word by sounding it out

*deep alphabetic orthography: a writing system that represents both phonemes and morphemes

*derivational suffix: a type of bound morpheme; a suffix— such as –ity, -ive, and -ly— that can change the part of speech of the root or base word to which it is added

dialects: mutually intelligible versions of the same language with systematic differences in phonology, word use, and/or grammatical rules

digraph: a two-letter combination that stands for a single phoneme in which neither letter represents its usual sound (ex. th, ph)

diphthong: a vowel produced by the tongue shifting position during articulation; a vowel that has a glide; a vowel that feels as if it has two parts, especially the vowels spelled ou and oi; some linguistics texts also classify all tense (long) vowels as diphthongs

direct instruction: instruction in which the teacher defines and teaches a concept, guides children through its application, and arranges for extended guided practice until mastery is achieved

dyslexia: an impairment of reading accuracy and fluency attributable to an underlying phonological deficit (see complete definition in Module 1)

*encoding: producing written symbols for spoken language; also, spelling by sounding out

*flap: the tongue rising behind the teeth to produce a diminished /t/ or /d/ in the middle of words such as water, better, little, and rudder

*fricative: a consonant sound created by forcing air through a narrow opening in the vocal tract; includes /f/, /v/, /s/, /z/, /sh/, /zh/, and /th/.

generalization: a pattern in the spelling system that applies to a substantial family of words

*glide: a type of speech sound that glides immediately into a vowel; includes /y/, /w/, and /h/

grapheme: a letter or letter combination that spells a phoneme; can be one, two, three, or four letters in English (ex. e, ei, igh, eigh)

inflection: a type of bound morpheme; a grammatical ending that does not change the part of speech of a word but that marks its tense, number, or degree in English (ex. -ed, -s, -ing)

integrated: lesson components that are interwoven and flow smoothly together

*lexicon: name for the mental dictionary in every person's linguistic processing system

*liquid: the speech sounds /l/ and /r/ that have vowel-like qualities and no easily definable point of articulation

logographic: a form of writing that represents the meaning of words and concepts with pictures or signs; contrasts with writing systems that represent speech sounds

long-term memory: the memory system that stores information beyond 24 hours

*marker: in linguistics, a letter that has no sound of its own but that indicates the sound of another letter or letter combination, such as the u in the word guard that makes the /g/ a hard sound

meaning processor: the neural networks that attach meanings to words that have been heard or decoded

*metalinguistic awareness: an acquired level of awareness of language structure and function that allows us to reflect on and consciously manipulate the language we use

Middle English: the form of English spoken between about 1200 and 1600—after the Norman invasion of England and before the time of Shakespeare

*monosyllabic: having one syllable

morpheme: the smallest meaningful unit of the language; it may be a word or part of a word; it may be one or more syllables, as in un-inter-rupt-able

morphology: the study of the meaningful units in the language and how they are combined in word formation

*morphophonemic: having to do with both sound and meaning

multisyllabic: having more than one syllable

narrative: text that tells about sequences of events, usually with the structure of a fiction or nonfiction story; often contrasted with expository text that reports factual information and the relationships among ideas

onset-rime: the natural division of a syllable into two parts, the onset coming before the vowel and the rime including the vowel and what follows it (pl-an, shr-ill)

orthographic processor: the neural networks responsible for perceiving, storing, and retrieving the letter sequences in words

orthography: a writing system for representing language

phoneme: a speech sound that combines with others in a language system to make words; English has 40 to 44 phonemes according to various linguists

phoneme awareness (also, phonemic awareness): the conscious awareness that words are made up of segments of our own speech that are represented with letters in an alphabetic orthography

phonics: the study of the relationships between letters and the sounds they represent; also used as a descriptor for code-based instruction in reading, i.e., "the phonics approach" or "phonic reading"

phonological awareness: meta-linguistic awareness of all levels of the speech sound system, including word boundaries, stress patterns, syllables, onset-rime units, and phonemes; a more encompassing term than phoneme awareness

phonological processor: a neural network in the frontal and temporal areas of the brain, usually the left cerebral hemisphere, that is specialized for speech sound perception, memory, retrieval, and pronunciation

phonological working memory: the "online" memory system that remembers speech long enough to extract meaning from it, or that holds onto words during writing; a function of the phonological processor

phonology: the rule system within a language by which phonemes can be sequenced, combined, and pronounced to make words

*pragmatics: the system of rules and conventions for using language and related gestures in a social context

prefix: a morpheme that precedes a root and that contributes to or modifies the meaning of a word; a common linguistic unit in Latin-based words

reading fluency: the speed of reading; the ability to read text with sufficient speed to support comprehension

root: a bound morpheme, usually of Latin origin, that cannot stand alone but that is used to form a family of words with related meanings

schwa: the "empty" vowel in an unaccented syllable, such as the last syllables of circus and bagel

semantics: the study of word and phrase meanings and relationships

*shallow alphabetic orthography: a writing system that represents speech sounds with letters directly and consistently, using one letter for each sound

silent letter spelling: a consonant grapheme with a silent letter and a letter that corresponds to the vocalized sound, such as kn, wr, and gn

sound-symbol correspondence: same as phoneme grapheme correspondence; the rules and patterns by which letters and letter combinations represent speech sounds

stop: a type of consonant that is spoken with one push of breath and not continued or carried out, including /p/, /b/, /t/, /d/, /k/, and /g/

structural analysis: the study of affixes, base words, and roots

suffix: a derivational morpheme (added to a root or base) that often changes the word's part of speech and modifies its meaning

*syllabic consonants: /m/, /n/, /l/, and /r/ can do the job of a vowel and make an unaccented syllable at the ends of words such as rhythm, mitten, little, and letter

syllable: the unit of pronunciation that is organized around a vowel; it may or may not have consonants before or after the vowel

vowel: one of a set of 15 vowel phonemes in English, not including vowel-r combinations; an open phoneme that is the nucleus of every syllable; classified by tongue position and height (high to low, front to back)

whole language: a philosophy of reading instruction that de-emphasizes the importance of phonics and phonology and that emphasizes the importance of learning to recognize words as wholes through encounters in meaningful contexts

word recognition: the instant recognition of a whole word in print

Appendix

Answers to Applicable Exercises

Exercise #1: Various Phonological Tasks

1. (Syllable Counting) How many syllables in each of the following words?

   cleaned __1__   poetic __3__   appreciated __5__   incredible __4__

2. (Rhyme Recognition) Do each of these word pairs rhyme (yes or no)? Speakers may differ in their judgments. *Answers vary. Words that are spelled differently can rhyme.*

   but, putt _____   been, when _____   loyal, toil _____

   merry, scary _____   on, yawn _____

3. (Word Pronunciation) How do you pronounce each of these words? On which ones might you reveal your regional or ethnic origins? *Answers vary.*

   tomato ☐   parker ☐   oil ☐   caught ☐   wash ☐   sing ☐

4. (Odd Word Out) Which word does not begin with the same sound as the others?

   theory ☐   therefore ☑   thistle ☐   thinker ☐

5. (Phoneme Matching). Which word has the same last sound as *does*?

   miss ☐   nice ☐   prize ☑   purchase ☐

6. (Initial Phoneme Isolation) Say the first speech sound in each of these words:

   europe /y/   chagrin /sh/   psychic /s/   question /k/

7. (Phoneme Blending) Blend these sounds together to make a whole, real word:

   /th/ /ŭ/ /m/ __thumb__   /s/ /t/ /ă/ /k/ /s/ __stacks__

   /m/ /or/ /f/ /ē/ /m/ __morpheme__   /y/ /ū/ /n/ /ə/ /v/ /er/ /s/ __universe__

8. (Phoneme Segmentation) Raise a finger for each sound as you break each word into its individual speech sounds (phonemes).

   shear   chains   quite   fleshy
   /sh/ /ē/ /r/   /ch/ /ā/ /n/ /z/ /k/ /w/ /ī/ /t/ /f/ /l/ /ĕ/ /sh/ /ē/

9. (Phoneme Deletion)

   Say *driver*. Say it again without the /v/.   __drier__

   Say *smoke*. Say it again without the /m/.   __soak__

   Say *sink*. Say it again without the /y/.   __sick__

   Say *six*. Say it again without the /k/.   __sis__

10. (Phoneme Sequence Identification) What is the third speech sound in each of these words?

    chunk /ng/   writhe /th/   vision /zh/   exit /s/

Exercise #3: Segmenting Words at Several Levels

How are these words divided? By syllable (S), onset-rime (O/R), or phoneme (P)?

h – ou – se	P	side – walk	S
f – igh – t	P	st – age	O/R
shr – imp	O/R	m – eat	O/R
an – i – mal	S	th – u – mb	P
po – ta – to	S	t – r – ee	P
air – plane	S	sh – oe	P

Exercise #4: Define the PH Words

Explain in your own words the distinctions among phonological processing, phoneme awareness, and phonics.

Phonological processing includes much more than phoneme awareness. It includes many functions and skills, such as remembering words, retrieving words from memory, comparing the sounds of words, counting syllables, rhyming, and breaking words into onsets and rimes.

Phoneme awareness is the ability to hear, identify, and manipulate the individual speech sounds in spoken words.

Phonics depends on phoneme awareness. It is only possible to learn the spellings for specific speech sounds in an alphabetic writing system such as English if those individual speech sounds can be differentiated and identified in spoken words.

Exercise #5: Count Phonemes in Words

Try counting the speech sounds in each of these words. Tap out the sounds with your thumb and fingers as you say them separately. We expect you to be unsure of some of the words!

   string __5__   joyless __5__   dodge __3__   mixed __5__   heard __3__

   hippo __4__   although __4__   chew __2__   house __3__

Exercise #6: Identify Beginning and Ending Consonants

Identify, say, and write the symbol for the consonant sounds that begin and end each word below. Don't be fooled by the word's spelling!

come	/k/, /m/	bridge	/b/, /j/	seethe	/s/, /th/
knob	/n/, /b/	crave	/k/, /v/	young	/y/, /ng/
cage	/k/, /j/	chaise	/sh/, /z/	rhyme	/r/, /m/
wrinkle	/r/, /l/	white	/wh/ or /w/, /t/	phone	/f/, /n/
one	/w/, /n/	united	/y/, /d/	gnat	/n/, /t/
thresh	/th/, /sh/	hymn	/h/, /m/	psychic	/s/, /k/
queen	/k/, /n/	rouge	/r/, /zh/	league	/l/, /g/
giant	/j/, /t/	whole	/h/, /l/	wage	/w/, /j/
rose	/r/, /z/	there	/th/, /r/	south	/s/, /th/

Exercise #10: Analyze Children's Writing

Look at these examples of children's writing. These children are spelling some words by sound, others by established sight word habits, and others by copying from a chart.

Identify the words that show:

1. Affrication of /t/ or /d/ so that it is changed to /ch/ or /j/.
2. Flapping of a medial /t/ so that it is changed to /d/.
3. Voiced/voiceless consonant substitution, or other substitution of consonants pronounced similarly.
4. Trouble with a consonant cluster (blend).
5. Substitution of vowels that are similar in articulation.
6. Omission of a nasal consonant after a vowel and before a consonant, or omission of /r/ or /l/ after a vowel.
7. Use of a single letter for a syllabic consonant /l/, /m/, or /r/.
8. Use of letter names to stand for specific phonemes (s, r).
9. Omission or confusion of inflected endings (e.g., -ed, -s, -ing).
10. Alternative letter possibility (silent e).

Sometime you can make pancakes with egg and with make and you can make pancakes with butte and grise.

—End of second grade

I was also frighten when i was going home and i was by lots of trees and it was lighting. I was so frightened by that. Sometime thing could be so frightened that you could jump out of your shoes. Things that are frightingly can scare you that you will not no what happened to you. I hate frightened things.

—End of fourth grade

I went to the birthday. Me and Cassd made ore bedroom into a hantd home. I shod my grem and grap.

—Beginning of first grade

---

transplant, strongest, unbleaded, quiet, anything, slender.

—Fourth grade spelling test result

I am gini bee a devil for halawene. I am going tric treting for Halawene. I fed the sdrae [stray] cat yesterday.

—Beginning of first grade

Then the witch came off her broomstc. Then the witch went over the bobrigh [drawbridge]. Then the witch noct on the door then the princess opind the door then the witch grab the princess and then the witct inagd that princess to her hows. Then a prince so the witch inagen the princss to her hows. Then the prince went after the witch bat the prince was to fat. Then the nixt dai the witch inagd the princss to a high town with no stars no dor.

—May of kindergarten*

* Child who had been taught through very systematic phonetic system, "Focus on Phonemes," by Pat Tyborowski (for more information, call 508-753-7551). The first three samples on the following page are also from children in that class.

A capuers [years] latr. The king did [died] then a witch came riden on the casl.

—Kindergarten

Once upon a time there was a princess and a prince and a dragin. The dragin poot the princess in a kaj. The prince rextyoud [rescued] the princess and livd hapulee evr after.

—Kindergarten

I am going to florlda and i will bring my bathing sut and a short sleve shrt and shorts. When i get there i will go and see micee mous and minee mous and then i will go to the bech.

—Kindergarten

Apirl hand lenkin worked at the white house

—End of kindergarten;
(child lives in Washington, D.C.)

73